JUDGES
MAKING
LAW

✳

JUDGES
MAKING
LAW

✳

EDWARD F. HENNESSEY

Copyright © 1994 by Franklin N. Flaschner Judicial Institute, Inc.
10 Winter Place, Boston, Massachusetts 02108

Library of Congress Cataloging-in-Publication Data

Hennessey, Edward F.
    Judges making law / by Edward F. Hennessey.
        p.   cm.
    Includes bibliographical references.
    ISBN 0-944394-01-9 (pbk.)
    1. Judges—United States.   2. Judicial process—United States.
    3. Jurisprudence—United States.   I. Title.
    KF8775.H46   1994
    347.73'14—dc20
    [347.30714]   94-48693
                                                                     CIP

ISBN 0-944394-01-9

Manufactured in the United States of America

[The Life of Chief Justice Marshall] stands for the rise of a new body of jurisprudence, by which guiding principles are raised above the reach of statute and state, and judges are entrusted with a solemn and hitherto unheard-of authority and duty.

—Justice Oliver Wendell Holmes, Jr.

Judges ought to be more learned than witty, more reverend than plausible, and more advised than confident. Above all things, integrity is their portion and proper virtue.

—Francis Bacon

A judge is bound to decide each case fairly, in accord with the relevant facts and the applicable law, even when the decision is not the one the home crowd wants.

—Chief Justice William H. Rehnquist

TABLE OF CONTENTS

FOREWORD

There are two reasons why I wrote this little book. First, and more important, I have looked back many years to the time when I was a litigating lawyer and the later time when I first became a judge, and I have thought about the kind of book which I could profitably have used then to learn some of the basics of judging. My second reason: for three successive years I have taught a law school course which has some resemblance to some courses called "Jurisprudence," "Judicial Process" and the like. I reviewed scores of excellent writings which treat judicial decision-making,[1] but I found no text which was a good fit with my teaching plan. Hence this volume.

Massachusetts cases are cited frequently in these pages. Measured in numbers only, without regard to complexity of the cases, various studies show that 95% to 98% of all litigation begins and ends in the state courts. Nevertheless, commentators more often than not concentrate on federal cases. Because this volume deals with process rather than substantive law, I feel confident in relying on Massachusetts cases as representative examples of the judicial process. In all of this I have attempted to bring into focus such insight as I have acquired from my years on the trial bench and appellate bench.

I proceed from the assumption that it is not a good thing for judges to make law according to their personal prejudices, philosophies and predilections. A continuing dialogue among judges and others has offered methods of judicial restraint and accountability in the common law, enacted law and constitutional law. A massive amount of scholarly writing is preoccupied with the search for objectivity in the judicial process.

---

[1] Four judges in particular have recently written unique and informative works about the decision-making process. See Coffin, "The Ways of a Judge" (1980); Keeton, "Judging" (1990); Posner, "The Problems of Jurisprudence" (1990); and Aldisert, "Logic for Lawyers" (1989). The writings of many other judges are cited in footnotes, *infra*.

Some have sought to identify consensus moral and ethical values, perhaps a futile pursuit in this multi-cultural society. (See n. 45, *infra.*) Many of these treatises are cited in the ensuing chapters of this volume. The unhappy fact is that many judges may read little of this scholarly material. Therefore, my emphasis throughout my discussion will be on those factors which I think judges themselves recognize as restraints upon their discretion. Necessarily, my limited selections among the mass of scholarly materials makes this book in one sense no more than a primer for its readers. I trust it is a useful primer.

The Flaschner Judicial Institute and the Charles H. Cross Charitable Foundation have generously provided funding for this publication, and have made it possible to distribute the work at a modest price.

I owe a great deal to Justice Rudolph Kass and Attorney Robert J. Brink for their suggestions in the final stages of this enterprise, and to Attorney Ieuan Mahony for his most valuable suggestions in the early stages of the writing. Most especially, I am grateful to Attorney Henry Clay for his vigilant monitoring from beginning to end.

EDWARD F. HENNESSEY
BOSTON, MASSACHUSETTS
JANUARY, 1994

Chapter One

SOME PRELIMINARY THOUGHTS

---

1. Judges as Lawmakers

This volume is concerned with the making of American law. We look at the common law, enacted (statute) law, and constitutional law. We consider both criminal and civil law. Our special interest is in the role of state and federal courts as lawmakers. We are not focusing on the substantive law; rather we look at the process. In this sense we are concerned with the brush strokes rather than the portrait.

Courts "make" law in all three areas: common law, enacted law and constitutional law. The proposition that judges merely find the law that was always there is a fiction. For example, it is seldom if ever possible to frame a universal rule of law, whether rooted in constitution or statute or common law, which will govern all controversies in a particular sphere. When a rule fails because of its generality, judges must make law to cover a specific situation. There are times also when judges determine that existing legal rules are not consistent with justice or the good of the community. It is then, when legal reasoning will not suffice, that judges make value judgments. It is in this discretionary exercise in making policy that judges most often are said to be legislating.

We shall find that concepts we discuss in one area of the law are applicable in another. We particularly observe similarity in reasoning in our discussions of the common law and constitutional law.

2. The Courts are Nonmajoritarian

Presidents and governors, and federal and state legislators, are elected. Federal judges are appointed for life. Some or all of the judges of fourteen states (at last count) are appointed, and never face the election process. Even as to "electing" states, judges first take office by executive appointment as judicial vacancies occur, and later must be elected to be retained in office. The elections in many states are not typical adversarial contests. For example, voters may be asked, in essence, to vote "yes" or "no" as to the judge's retention. Even where the adversarial process is fully observed in electing judges, it is unlikely that the electorate are

---

content to be governed by a "legislature" of seven or nine persons. A court's holdings in the common law or statutory interpretation may be negated with relative speed by legislative action. Nevertheless, all things considered, the courts are nonmajoritarian, and are regarded as such.

The nonmajoritarian nature of the courts may constitute their greatest value. Historically, the role of the American courts has been explained in undemocratic terms. It is premised that, if the courts were fully responsive to the electoral process, there would be an erosion of the rights, especially constitutional rights, of some persons and classes of persons. In light of this it may be incongruous for some to assert, as we shall see later, that the courts in policy decisions shall be responsive to the will of the community. Protection of individual rights may, as often as not, be inconsistent with the will of the majority in the community.

3. The Courts and Institutional Legitimacy

Because the courts make law and because they are nonmajoritarian, what is the legitimacy of the courts as an institution? Is there an identifiable and limited role for the courts, and if there is such a role, how far may the courts step outside that role and remain legitimate? Especially in those cases where precedent and legal reasoning fail, and policy must be established, where do courts get the values (social, economic, moral and political) which determine policy? These are crucial questions, and undoubtedly will remain so as long as our form of government survives, because opposition to any decision of a court may focus not only on the merits but on the doubtful source of the court's power.

This volume is not intended to be a broadside of adverse criticism of judges as lawmakers, because we have in mind that, in usual course, courts do not act with intrusive volunteerism. However, judges must decide the cases brought before them and in so doing they encounter the inevitable tensions inherent in the American system. At various places in the ensuing pages, I refer to these tensions, and I summarize some of them in the final chapter of this volume, in the section called "Permanent Tensions."

This volume focuses to a great extent on what courts do at the limits of the law where the legitimacy of the court's action may be in question. We point out that the court as an institution is not good at discovering the popular mindset. Because, unlike a legislature, a court is not institutionally equipped to discover the will of the people, the subjective whim of the judge may control at the edges of the law. It is in these areas that the legitimacy of the court is problematic, and the wise judge uses self-restraint.

Because of our focus on the edges of the law, it is probably useful here to describe the center of the law where the court's legitimacy is most certain. The edges of the law are rarified and ordinarily are for the court of ultimate jurisdiction only. A trial court judge and an intermediate appellate court judge, as well as the attorneys who practice before them, should have a clear idea of the unquestionably legitimate role of the court. This role centers on what judges are institutionally equipped to do: reasoning from precedent based on the facts before them using traditional tools. See Chapter Two, Sec. 3, "Judicial Restraint: Legal Reasoning."

4. Some Important Terms

We analyze at length, in Chapters Three and Four, various schools of thought concerning statutory and constitutional construction. It may be helpful to arrange in definitional groups the most important of the terminology. See also Chapter Five, Sec. 1, "Permanent Tensions."

In reference to "strict construction," commonly espoused by those who are conservative in politics or legal philosophy, we can group together: interpretivists, literalists, formalists, and textualists.

In reference to "loose construction," commonly supported by those who are liberal in politics or legal philosophy, we can group together: non-interpretivists, institutionalists, and realists. Some writers are fond of the term "originalists," in this category.

Some writers use the terms in each group interchangeably.

Chapter Two

THE COMMON LAW

---

1. What is the Common Law?

The common law is that body of law which emanates from court decisions, rather than from statutes or constitutions. The common law is distinguished from the "civil law" of some European and Latin American countries, where the sole source of law is limited, at least in theory, to codes and statutes.

Common law is subordinate to legislative enactments, but both common law and enacted law are subordinate to constitutional law.

Unlike statute law, which ordinarily applies prospectively, common law rules ordinarily apply retroactively, and apply to the very case that prompted the rule-making.

The common law inevitably at times intersects with constitutions, in that judge-made law must be responsive to constitutional limits. The common law also intersects with statutes, in that it frequently fleshes out the generalities of statutes. This latter function may go beyond the process of judicial interpretation of statutory meanings, because the legislature may use generality of wording in the statutes in the knowledge that the court will supplement the statutes with common law concepts. For example, in many states the criminal statutes are written in the framework and context of the common law.[2]

Similarly, a federal common law has arisen as intended by Congress. There is a widespread misunderstanding that all common law is state law. To the contrary, the federal courts make a large body of common law.[3] In the eighteenth and nineteenth centuries a body of judge-made law arose in many cases which were in the federal courts solely by reason

---

[2] See *Commonwealth* v. *Cass*, 392 Mass. 799, 801-807 (1984), for a discussion of this interrelationship.

[3] Not everyone agrees that there is federal common law. Presumably some would call all such rulings "interpretation" of the statute. See, e.g., Wilkinson, "The Role of Reason in the Rule of Law," 56 U. Chi. L. Rev. 779 (1989). In discussing reasoning by federal judges, Judge Wilkinson says: "The legal universe is the handiwork of others: judge-made law, as such, has no place."

of diversity of citizenship. This body of law was institutionalized in *Swift* v. *Tyson*, 41 U.S. 1 (1842). However, the *Swift* case was overruled as a federal usurpation of state power by *Erie Railroad Co.* v. *Tompkins*, 304 U.S. 64 (1938).

The *Erie* principle has not prevented the creation of a large area of federal law which can only be called common law. The Congress, like state legislatures, has used generality of language in a number of statutes with the clearly implied intention that judge-made law should be a supplement.[4] Examples: The Sherman Anti-Trust Act;[5] National Labor Relations Act;[6] Civil Rights Act of 1866;[7] Securities Act of 1933 and Securities Exchange Act of 1934;[8] and the Voting Rights Act.[9]

From the federal constitution and state constitutions, directly or indirectly, have also come large areas of law made by the courts in giving substance to general terms.[10] These areas are illustrative of the similarities between common law and constitutional reasoning and, at the same time, are at the center of the tension between strict and liberal construction of constitutional language.

2. The Common Law and Judicial Restraint

In the deliberations of judges there is a constant internal pressure toward

---

[4]*National Soc'y of Professional Eng'rs* v. *United States*, 435 U.S. 679, 688 (1978) ("Congress . . . did not intend the text of the . . . Act to delineate the full meaning of the statute or its application in concrete situations. The legislative history makes it perfectly clear that it expected the courts to give shape to the statute's broad mandate by drawing on common law tradition").

[5] 15 U. S. C. §§ 1-7 (1990).

[6] 29 U. S. C. § 151 et seq (1982).

[7] 42 U. S. C. § 1981 et seq (1982).

[8] 15 U. S. C. § 77a et seq (1987); 15 U. S. C. § 78a et seq (1990).

[9] Voting Rights Act of 1965, § 2 (b), 42 U. S. C. § 1973 (1982).

[10] Some examples from the federal Constitution:

First Amendment -	"establishment of religion"
	"free exercise" (of religion)
	"freedom of speech"
	(freedom) "of the press"
Fourth Amendment -	"unreasonable" (search and seizure)
Fifth Amendment -	"witness against himself"
	"due process of law"
Sixth Amendment -	"speedy and public trial"
	"assistance of counsel"
Eighth Amendment -	"cruel and unusual" (punishment)
Fourteenth Amendment -	"due process of law"
	"equal protection of the laws"

---

subjective thinking. Justice Cardozo recognized this, but emphasized that personal convictions have validity only after legal analysis has been tried and fails ("when reasons are nicely balanced"): "All their lives forces which the [judges] do not recognize and cannot name have been tugging at them—inherited instincts, traditional beliefs, acquired convictions; and the resultant is an outlook on life, a conception of social needs, a sense in James's phrase of 'the total push and pressure of the cosmos,' which, when reasons are nicely balanced, must determine where choice shall fall. In this mental background every problem finds its setting. We may try to see things as objectively as we please. None the less, we can never see them with any eyes except our own. To that test they are all brought—a form of pleading or an act of parliament, the wrongs of paupers or the rights of princes, a village ordinance or a nation's charter."[11]

Along parallel lines, Professor Paul Freund has written that judges should invoke personal convictions and values only in the case of necessity: "Much of law is designed to avoid the necessity for the judge to reach what Holmes called his 'can't helps,' his ultimate convictions or values. The force of precedent, the close applicability of statute law, the separation of powers, legal preemptions, statutes of limitations, rules of pleading and evidence, and above all the pragmatic assessments of fact that point to one result whichever ultimate values be assumed, all enable the judge in most cases to stop short of a resort to his personal standards. When these prove unavailing, as is more likely in the case of courts of last resort at the frontiers of the law, the most likely in a supreme constitutional court, the judge necessarily resorts to his own scheme of values. It may therefore be said that the most important thing about a judge is his philosophy; and if it be dangerous for him to have one, it is at all events less dangerous than the self-deception of having none."[12]

Freund and Cardozo, and many others, have thus urged restraint in the judge's resort to personal values. Many writers, as we shall see later in our discussion of "Value Judgments and Policy Decisions," have also urged that the values and policies sought by the judge should be, not her own, but those of the community.[13]

---

[11] Cardozo, "The Nature of the Judicial Process," 12, 13 (1921).

[12] Freund, "Social Justice," 93, 110 (R. Brandt ed. 1962).

[13] See, e.g., n.45 *infra*.

3. Judicial Restraint: Legal Reasoning

We turn now to a discussion of legal reasoning as a restraint upon judges in their common law exercise. Unlike the legislature, which need not include words of justification within a new statute, the appellate court usually seeks to justify its results with reasoning. It is legal reasoning which establishes, or fails to establish, acceptance of the court's action,[14] and it is legal reasoning which tends to support the growth of the common law incrementally, rather than peremptorily. The reasoning may be a target of comment and criticism, and there is no question that appellate judges as they write are alert to the prospect of dissenting opinions, as well as adverse criticism from the bench and the bar, and from legal periodicals and the news media.

Legal reasoning is a phrase under which we group some of the concepts which restrain and discipline the judicial process, and a phrase which is often used, but seldom defined, or even definitively illustrated, by writers on jurisprudence. Legal reasoning in support of common law decisions is similar in kind to "neutral principles" urged by some as necessary to validate decisions in constitutional interpretation.[15] Professor Freund listed a number of ingredients for legal reasoning in our quotation from him above. See n.12 *supra*. We shall see many aspects of legal reasoning in our discussions below of stare decisis and analogy, in the inductive and deductive nature of the growth of the law, in the separation of powers, in the balancing of interests and values, and the effect or close applicability of statutes upon the common law.

A court in its reasoning may rely on the constitutional principles of separation of powers. This is a major restraint upon the direction of the common law. Common law rules must be constitutional and may not contradict a statute, if the statute is constitutional. Even when there is no direct contradiction, the court may accept the guidance of a policy

---

[14] Not all scholars agree that legal reasoning, however adroit, supports acceptance of a court's decision. Some Critical Legal Studies advocates say that legal reasoning is simply a rationale to support the preferences of those in power, that legal thought in any given case can be adjusted to give credible support to almost any result, and that legal reasoning and political dialogue are indistinguishable. See generally, Hutchinson and Monahan, "Law Politics and the Critical Legal Scholars: The Unfolding Drama of American Legal Thought," 36 Stan. L. Rev. 199 (1984); Unger, "The Critical Legal Studies Movement" (1986); see n.166 *infra*.

[15] See, e.g., Wechsler, "Toward Neutral Principles of Constitutional Law," 73 Harv. L. Rev. 1 (1959). We discuss neutral principles in our chapter on constitutional law. The analogy should not be extended too far, because the neutral principles in constitutional law include, of course, a legal text, a constitution.

established by the legislature in analogous matters,[16] or the court in its discretion may decline to act in the common law when it deems legislative action is preferable.[17]

The common-law courts are equally responsive to restraints which do not come from constitutions or statutes, but are self-imposed. These constitute the most common ingredients of legal reasoning, and we include them in the following discussion of judicial restraint.

4. Judicial Restraint: Incremental Growth

Jurists and legal scholars agree that the common law has grown incrementally, and they also agree that this is as it should be.[18] Many American judges may never have read the work of Holmes, or any other jurisprudential writings, but there was early on a general understanding among judges that the common law evolves by accretion. Judge Cardozo wrote that the law is rooted in history, custom, logic (philosophy) and sociology.[19] The first three ingredients are clearly supportive of incremental growth of the common law; we discuss the special characteristics of the fourth factor, sociology, later in our comments on value judgments.

The incremental growth of the law is illustrated by a series of actions in contract successfully pursued by employees at will who had been discharged without good cause.[20] Movement toward an expansion of former employees' rights has been gradual and perhaps not yet totally defined. These analogous cases focus on public policy, like the *Stamboulis*

---

[16] See *DiLuzio v. United Elec. Radio & Mach.Workers of Am., Local 274*, 386 Mass. 314, 325 n.2, 318 and n.5 (1982); and *Knowles v. Gilchrist Co.*, 362 Mass. 642, 643, 651-652 (1972).

[17] See, e.g., *Whitney v. Worcester*, 373 Mass. 208, 209-212 (1977).

[18] See, e.g., Holmes, "The Path of the Law," 10 Harv. L. Rev. 457, 468 (1897).

[19] Cardozo, "The Nature of the Judicial Process," 30-31 (1921). Cardozo states that custom may be confined to an industry or profession, to a particular locality, or may have widespread or general significance.

[20] See *Fortune v. National Cash Register Co.*, 373 Mass. 96, 104, 105 (1977) (employee discharged without cause and in bad faith to avoid paying him commissions); *Gram v. Liberty Mut. Ins. Co.*, 384 Mass. 659, 671-674 (1981) (employee discharged without cause and without bad faith entitled to recover future commissions for past services); *DeRose v. Putnam Management Co.*, 398 Mass. 205, 210-211 (1986) (employee recovers where, contrary to public policy, he is discharged for failing to testify in criminal proceeding in accordance with employer's suggestion). See also *Cort v. Bristol-Myers Co.*, 385 Mass. 300, 303-310 (1982); *Federici v. Mansfield Credit Union*, 399 Mass. 592, 594-597 (1987); *Flesner v. Technical Communications Corp.*, 410 Mass. 805 (1991); and *Wright v. Shriners Hosp. for Crippled Children*, 412 Mass. 469 (1992).

---

case, *infra*, n.27, and, like *Stamboulis*, may be moving toward a statement of principle which embraces them all.

A similar instance of incremental movements occurred after the legislature abrogated governmental immunity and, in substance, left to the courts the striking of an appropriate balance between the public interest in fairness to injured persons and in promoting effective government. The court in a series of cases denied relief when the governmental entity committed a breach of duty owed to the general public.[21] In other cases the court granted relief where there was a special relationship between the plaintiff and the defendant.[22] As shown, *infra*, in our discussion of inductive reasoning, the cases illustrate the desirability, as well as the difficulty, of identifying and extracting a controlling principle.[23]

In the face of the methodology of gradual accretion of the common law, the role of scholarly writings, particularly from legal study organizations like the American Law Institute, is an uncertain one. These sources are especially valuable when legal reasoning is sparse and their support adds strength.

5. Judicial Restraint: Stare Decisis; Deductive and Inductive Reasoning

The doctrine of stare decisis is the major judge-made control over judges' decisions. Adherence to precedent is a factor that promotes confidence in the continuity of the law. A basic ingredient, inherent in the concept of stare decisis, is that American courts in a given jurisdiction must adhere to precedents established by courts of superior position in the hierarchy of the jurisdiction. Thus ultimate precedential authority in some instances resides in the Supreme Court of the United States, and in other instances in the highest court of a state.

The doctrine of stare decisis is simply stated: the material facts of an earlier case are examined and if they are identical or similar to the

---

[21] *Dinsky* v. *Framingham*, 386 Mass. 801 (1982); *Nickerson* v. *Commonwealth*, 397 Mass. 476 (1986); *Appleton* v. *Hudson*, 397 Mass. 812 (1986); *Patrazza* v. *Commonwealth*, 398 Mass. 464 (1986).

[22] *Irwin* v. *Ware*, 392 Mass. 745 (1984); *A.L.* v. *Commonwealth*, 402 Mass. 234 (1988).

[23] In *Jean W.* v. *Commonwealth*, 414 Mass. 496 (1993), a divided court offers various approaches toward a controlling line-drawing principle for governmental liability, and a majority announce an intention to abandon the "public duty" rule of governmental immunity.

case at issue, the decision of the earlier matter stands as precedent for the later case.

The process is thus a deductive one.[24] Each decision is influenced by the precedent of earlier cases with similar facts, and the rule of the decision reaches no farther than the facts of the case.

But the process is also inductive.[25] From related decisions, a concept broader than the rule of any one case may evolve. This inclusive concept has been called by some, not merely a rule, but a doctrine or principle. Whatever its name, the new concept is supported by inductive reasoning. The process now looks to consequences rather than antecedents.

For example, the high court of Massachusetts over a period of twenty years decided a pattern of cases concerning the "status" of parties in tort actions.[26] Subsequently, in a case where a minor child sued his

---

[24]**The Syllogism**

The syllogism is a reasoning process common in problems of logic. The syllogism is inherent in legal arguments but, more often than not, is not specifically set forth. Rather it is urged by implication.

See Aldisert, "Logic for Lawyers" (1989) for a comprehensive discussion of the place of the syllogism in legal reasoning. The categorical syllogism, most frequently used in legal argument, consists of a major premise, a minor premise, and a conclusion.

major premise:	all dogs are carnivorous
minor premise:	Fido is a dog
conclusion:	Fido is carnivorous

Applying the teaching of Cardozo, we answer the question, "Where does the major premise come from?" Cardozo tells us that it comes from history, custom, logic (philosophy) or sociology. Logic (philosophy) includes the processes of deductive and inductive reasoning.

For examples of sub-syllogisms "folded into" a parent syllogism, see McFadden, "The Balancing Test," 29 B.C.L. Rev. 585, 589 (1988).

[25] A simple example of inductive reasoning:

Black Beauty (a horse) has four legs			
Man O'War	"	"	"
Citation	"	"	"
Silver	"	"	"
Trigger	"	"	"
Secretariat	"	"	"
Dan Patch	"	"	"

Conclusion: all horses have four legs.

[26] See *Colby* v. *Carney Hosp.*, 356 Mass. 527, 528 (1969) (defendant's status as a charity not to be a bar to liability in future cases); *Mounsey* v. *Ellard*, 363 Mass. 693, 707 (1973) (landowner's duty of care not affected by status of person lawfully on the premises); *Lewis* v. *Lewis*, 370 Mass. 619, 629-630 (1976) (interspousal immunity abolished as to motor vehicle accidents); *Whitney* v. *Worcester*, 373 Mass. 208, 210 (1977) (common law governmental immunity to be abrogated); *Brown* v. *Brown*, 381 Mass. 231, 231 (1980) (interspousal immunity abolished as to nonmotor vehicle torts).

---

parents, the court, relying on all of these status cases, announced the "principle" that the status of a party is not a controlling element in determining liability for negligence.[27]

In applying inductive reasoning, it is usually futile to attempt to state a principle of law from one or a few examples. Consider the *Manning* case where a defendant was charged with a minor offense related to illegal drugs, and police officers willfully interfered with his constitutional rights to counsel and a fair trial. The court dismissed the indictment with prejudice, relying, in part at least, upon the prophylactic effect of the decision in preventing similar flagrant overreaching by police.[28] But what if, in subsequent cases, the police misconduct is just as reprehensible as that in *Manning*, but the offense charged is murder, rather than a minor drug crime? In such instances, the court has declined to dismiss the indictments and declined to follow what may have appeared in *Manning* to be the establishment of a concept of broad application.[29]

The principle which is extracted by inductive reasoning is the major premise for deductive reasoning in deciding future cases. However, it does not have finality, nor should it have. Inductive reasoning proceeds by analogy and for that reason its conclusion states no more than a probability, although the probability may be to a high degree.[30] New analogous cases may arise which modify or even demolish the principle. Thus the common law principle of governmental immunity, which had existed for generations, was struck down after an examination of the many exceptions which had been created to avoid the injustice of the principle.[31]

Another example of principles demolished: landlord and tenant relationships were controlled for generations by the existence of independent covenants and the principle that a lease was a conveyance of an estate in real property for a term. The court, relying on common law

---

[27] *Stamboulis* v. *Stamboulis*, 401 Mass. 762, 764, 765 (1988).

[28] *Commonwealth* v. *Manning*, 373 Mass. 438, 443-445 (1977).

[29] *Commonwealth* v. *Hine*, 393 Mass. 564, 570-573 (1984) (defendant charged with murder; police forged defendant's signature on *Miranda* warning card); *Commonwealth* v. *Lewin*, 405 Mass. 566, 585-588 (1989) (defendant charged with murder; police committed perjury in testimony).

[30] Judge Aldisert in his book "Logic for Lawyers," *supra* n.24, offers that one might, by inductive reasoning, conclude that all swans are white in color, until one visited Australia and discovered black swans.

[31] *Whitney* v. *Worcester*, 373 Mass. 208, 225-226 (1977); see *Morash & Sons, Inc.* v. *Commonwealth*, 363 Mass. 612, 623, 624 (1973).

developments in other jurisdictions, determined that this principle had outlived its usefulness and that the modern view of the law recognizes a lease of a residence as essentially a contract between a landlord and a tenant in which the landlord promises to deliver and maintain the demised premises in a habitable condition and the tenant promises to pay rent for such premises, and their promises are interdependent.[32]

Similarly, upon re-examination of its long-standing felony-murder rules, the court, after looking to the law of other jurisdictions, established for the first time that a felony-murder conviction could be sustained only if, upon appropriate evidence and instructions, the jury determined that the defendant consciously disregarded the risk to human life.[33]

Principles may come into conflict. One principle may point to one conclusion; other principles may point with equal certainty to another. In that instance the court must choose one path or the other, or perhaps a third which is recommended by the force of the two principles in combination. For example, consider the case of a legatee who murdered his testator. The court was faced with conflict between established principles of law. There was the binding force of the will disposing of the estate of a testator in conformity with law. Against this was the deeply rooted principle that no person should profit from his or her own wrong. In this case, the latter principle prevailed.[34]

In the foregoing discussion of legal reasoning we have observed a number of instances where the court, in establishing a principle of common law, of necessity decided issues of policy and value judgment. We next discuss the discretionary choice of policies and values.

6. Value Judgments and Policy Decisions; The Balancing Process

It is necessary for the common law to grow, and the overriding considerations are justice and the good of the community. The necessity for growth often requires the court to reach value judgments. Objectivity in the process is especially difficult at these junctures.

We have seen that Judge Cardozo, in his discussion of the sources of the common law, named history, custom, logic (philosophy), and sociology.[35] The first three we have treated as components of legal

---

[32]*Boston Hous. Auth.* v. *Hemingway*, 363 Mass. 184, 196-199 (1973).

[33]*Commonwealth* v. *Matchett*, 386 Mass. 492, 508 (1982).

[34]*Riggs* v. *Palmer*, 115 N.Y. 506 (1889).

[35]Cardozo, "The Nature of the Judicial Process," 30, 31 (1921).

reasoning. His reference to "sociology" applies to a court's approach to policy decisions when legal reasoning will not suffice.

The school of thought supported by the "Realists" warned against undue reliance on legal reasoning. "The nadir of mechanical jurisprudence is reached when conceptions are used, not as premises from which to reason, but as ultimate solutions. So used, they cease to be conceptions and become empty words."[36]

Clearly the court makes a discretionary policy decision when it decides a case of first instance, where there exists little or no legal reasoning as we have defined it.[37] Also, in our preceding discussions we have shown many other instances of policy decisions. We have seen, for example, that the court in its discretion may identify and adopt a principle of law from the precedents, or it may decline to recognize a principle on the premise that precedents and legal reasoning are leading in a direction that is not in the public interest, or it may modify or even abolish a recognized principle. It is in making these choices that the court is acting most like a legislature, and Cardozo has said that the court is venturing into "sociology." The reasoning of the court is not legal in nature, but political, in the sense that the court marshalls and presents the rationale that a legislative advocate might offer on an issue of public policy.[38]

There is no question that the courts, in making common law policy decisions, engage in a balancing process, weighing and comparing competing values and interests.[39] The balancing may be reflected in the briefs of counsel, and the reasoning of the courts' opinions.

In these sociological ventures the court, the nonmajoritarian branch of government, can claim no special expertise or wisdom as to what is best for the community. It is then that the institutional integrity of the court is particularly subject to challenge, and the wisdom of the court's views may be at issue. As to legal reasoning that may be leading the court falsely, Holmes has said that "the law is administered by able and

---

[36] Pound, "Mechanical Jurisprudence," 8 Colum. L. Rev. 605, 620-621 (1908).

[37] See, e.g., *Dinsky* v. *Framingham*, 386 Mass. 801 (1982); *Irwin* v. *Ware*, 392 Mass. 745 (1984).

[38] See, for example, *Payton* v. *Abbott Labs.*, 386 Mass. 540, 564-570 (1982) (Hennessey, C.J., dissenting); *Ferriter* v. *Daniel O'Connell's Sons, Inc.*, 381 Mass. 507 (1980), (Quirico, J., concurring in part, Hennessey, C.J., dissenting, Wilkins, J., dissenting); *Dziokonski* v. *Babineau*, 375 Mass. 555 (1978) (Quirico, J., dissenting); and *Diaz* v. *Eli Lilly & Co.*, 364 Mass. 153 (1973).

[39] See generally, McFadden, "The Balancing Test," 29 B.C.L. Rev. 585 (1988).

---

experienced [judges]" who, in establishing public policy, "know too much to sacrifice good sense to a syllogism."[40] However, there may be controversy as to where good sense lies, as shown, for example, in *Commonwealth* v. *Grey*.[41] The Massachusetts court had established a long-standing principle that partial responsibility or diminished mental capacity of the defendant, short of insanity, is not relevant in the trial of most criminal cases.[42] The court, adhering to the incremental legal reasoning of a series of cases, has now established that mental abnormality is relevant as to crimes of specific intent.[43] The dissent in Grey opined that the community is not well served by legal reasoning, however orderly and syllogistic, which now requires the jury to consider, among other things, as bearing on the issue of the guilt of the defendant in cases of second degree murder, armed robbery, and other crimes of violence, whether the defendant was intoxicated by voluntary use of alcohol or drugs.[44]

Some writers urge that any policy or value judgment expressed by the court should be congruent with the thinking of the community as a whole, or in substantial part. But a consensus view, or even a majority view, may be hard to identify in our multi-cultural country. Further, how is the court, the most isolated of institutions, to discover the popular mind set? Most of the sources of information readily available to the legislature are barred to the court. The conversation of the judge's acquaintances or the comments of the news media may not be representative or even relevant. Therein lies one of the tensions in the judicial process: that the common law should not only grow in directions good for the community, but also should be accepted by the community, or at least by its informed members. "This, in the end, is how and why judicial review is consistent with the theory and practice of political democracy."[45] But in the minds of the judges the two goals may not

---

[40] Holmes, "The Common Law" 36 (1881).

[41] 399 Mass. 469 (1987).

[42] See, e.g., *Commonwealth* v. *Delle Chiaie*, 323 Mass. 615, 617-618 (1949); *Commonwealth* v. *Taylor*, 263 Mass. 356, 362-363 (1928).

[43] See *Commonwealth* v. *Mazza*, 366 Mass. 30, 34 (1974); *Commonwealth* v. *Gould*, 380 Mass. 672, 685 (1980); *Commonwealth* v. *Perry*, 385 Mass. 639, 648 (1982); *Commonwealth* v. *Loretta*, 386 Mass. 794, 799-800 (1982); *Commonwealth* v. *Henson*, 394 Mass. 584, 592-594 (1985).

[44] 399 Mass. 469, 475-478.

[45] Bickel, "The Least Dangerous Branch," 258 (2d ed. 1962); Eisenberg, "The Nature of the Common Law," 29 (1988); O'Connell, "Taking Process Seriously in Judicial Decision-Making," 67 OR. L.Rev. 837, 838-840 (1988).

---

be congruent. In this aspect, as in many others, judicial process in the common law is similar to that in constitutional law.

7. Discretion of the Trial Judge

Our discussion in this volume most often refers to law-making by the appellate courts. Nevertheless, it is important to consider the trial judge's function. Is the trial judge, like the appellate court, a lawmaker? Is there in every case a correct or "right" answer, by application of the law to the facts? Are trial judges well and truly applying constitutional law, statute law and common law?

We have observed that the trial judge is bound by the legal precedents established in the judicial hierarchy in which she participates. Consider the hypothesis that a trial judge is determined to implement her personal social philosophy at every opportunity, even disregarding applicable rules of law. This thesis subordinates principles of law to sociological considerations, and our hypothetical trial judge who is motivated solely toward social reform, and disregards applicable law, becomes a self-appointed legislator. Reversible error by the trial judge in many instances may be shown on appeal, as in rulings on evidence, motions for judgment addressed to insufficiency of the evidence, instructions to the jury, and many other rulings on questions of law. However, our hypothesis is not far-fetched, because a judge in many instances may disregard applicable rules of law without discernible error.

There also are a great many instances where decisions are discretionary, and there can be no error, because there is no "right" answer. It is particularly in these areas that the personal philosophy of the judge may be exerted with little or no restraint.[46] For example, there are the cases of first instance, where there are no relevant precedents. There also are the vast number of issues which the appellate courts have said are to be decided on a case by case basis.[47] Other examples are decisions on discovery, sanctions, injunctions, and sentencing and probation. In these

---

[46]Wilkinson, "The Role of Reason in the Rule of Law," 56 U. Chi. L. Rev. 779, 781 (1989).

[47]See Scalia, "The Rule of Law as a Law of Rules," 56 U. Chi. L. Rev. 1175 (1989), wherein the author expresses his reasons why he regrets the large number of issues that are to be decided case by case. See also *Salamanca* v. *United States*, 316 U.S. 694 (1942); *Curtis* v. *Commissioner*, 623 F.2d 1047 (5th Cir. 1980); and *United States* v. *Forness*, 125 F.2d 928, 942 (2d Cir.), all for the point that consistency in applying the law may be best supported, not by mere recitation of a standard of review (e.g., "clear and convincing evidence") but rather by requiring trial judges to make findings in meticulous detail.

and many other matters where the judge sits as fact-finder without a jury (e.g., motions to suppress evidence in criminal proceedings) her personal philosophy may be supported (we assume without loss of integrity) by her choice of findings as to the credibility of evidence.

As to the areas where discretion has been conferred, external controls are limited. The appellate court or the legislature may have instituted criteria for the exercise of discretion, but these require only that the judge consider them. Examples are sentencing "guidelines," requisite considerations as to injunctions, motions for new trials, and criteria for the division of marital assets after divorce. The applicable standard of review is "abuse of discretion," "clearly erroneous," or similar phrase, and appellate reversals on that basis are rare indeed. Within these loose restraints there is much room for what judges and legal scholars have referred to as the judge's "hunch" or "intuition."[48] This phenomenon, although pretty much immeasurable as to its precise impact upon the community, undoubtedly has great influence upon the operative effect of legal principles of the constitutions, the statutes and the common law.

The trial judge's role in the growth of the common law may be especially influential in any case where the established rules of law are not a good fit with the facts of the case. In deciding the case, the trial judge may reshape the law, and on appeal the result may be memorialized.

---

[48]Judge Hutcheson, in his article "The Judgment Intuitive: the Function of the 'Hunch' in Judicial Decisions," 14 Cornell L. Q. 274, 278 (1919), described the judicial hunch as follows: "I, after canvassing all the available market at my command, and duly cogitating upon it, give my imagination play, and brooding over the cause, wait for the feeling, the hunch - that intuitive flash of understanding which makes the jump spark connection between question and decision, and at the point where the path is darkest for the judicial feet, sheds its light along the way." See also Yablon, "Justifying the Judge's Hunch: An Essay on Discretion," 41 Hastings L.J. 231 (1990).

Chapter Three

ENACTED LAW

---

1. Introduction

In this chapter we consider the courts' function in construing statutes. The courts' task is to interpret the will of the enacting legislature.

State and federal law reports are replete with cases which illustrate the serious and extraordinarily difficult problem of statutory construction.

The Mann Act of 1910, entitled by Congress "The White Slave Traffic Act,"[49] is a striking example of a controversial history of judicial construction. The Act provided in part: "...[A]ny person who shall knowingly transport or cause to be transported, or aid or assist in obtaining transportation for, or in transporting, in interstate or foreign commerce or in any territory or in the District of Columbia, any woman or girl for the purpose of prostitution or debauchery, or for any other immoral purpose, or with the intent and purpose to induce, entice or compel such woman or girl to become a prostitute, or to give herself up to debauchery, or to engage in any other immoral practice...shall be deemed guilty of a felony."

A strong but certainly not conclusive argument has been made, from the Mann Act's language and legislative history, that Congress intended to combat organized interstate traffic in prostitution. Nevertheless, by reason of the ambiguity of the Act, criminal convictions and jail sentences have resulted where there was no showing of organized traffic,[50] enslave-

---

[49] 36 Stat. 825 (1910). See the comprehensive analysis of the Act, and its construction by the courts, in Levi, "An Introduction to Legal Reasoning" (1949).

[50] *Caminetti* v. *United States*, 242 U.S. 470 (1917).

ment of women,[51] or even prostitution.[52]

More recently, the Racketeer Influenced and Corrupt Organizations Act (RICO)[53] has caused sharp debate among lawyers and widely divergent views of the Justices of the Supreme Court, as to the intent of Congress. RICO takes aim at "racketeering activity." As with the Mann Act, a compelling case can be made that Congress meant to attack organized crime.[54] However, the Act has swept broadly as applied by the courts, to cover a variety of crimes and civil cases which had no connection to organized crime. In reversing a judgment in a civil case that RICO applies only to litigants who have been convicted of crimes related to the civil litigation, it appeared that the Justices of the Supreme Court were unanimously of the view that Congress did not intend the consequences which were occurring in RICO litigation, but a majority of the Justices were of the view that only Congress could correct the abuses under the statute.[55]

There are any number of other examples of statutory constructions by the courts which have caused sharp, even bitter, disputes in divided courts and among commentators and litigants. A few examples of far-reaching decisions: a case which rejected the claims of many service men and women under the Federal Tort Claims Act;[56] a case which restricted the rights of certain litigants in civil rights actions;[57] and a case which restricted the privileges of medical personnel to give abortion advice to women at federally-supported clinics.[58]

State and federal courts have been in recent decades increasingly occupied with statutory interpretation, to the point where the great majority of cases now involve statutes. The work of American legislatures has been a piecemeal process, with statutes narrow in their reach, for the most part, as distinguished from the comprehensive products enacted in civil code countries.

---

[51] See, e.g., *United States v. Holte*, 236 U.S. 140 (1915); *Cleveland v. United States*, 329 U.S. 14 (1946).

[52] See, e.g., *Athanasaw v. United States*, 227 U.S. 326 (1913) (amorous advances sufficient for conviction).

[53] 18 U.S.C. §§ 1961-1968 (1970).

[54] See "The Rico Racket," National Legal Center for the Public Interest (1989) for collection of relevant cases in the various essays presented.

[55] *Sedima, S.P.R.L. v. Imrex Co.*, Inc., 473 U.S. 479, 499-500 (1985).

[56] *Feres v. United States*, 340 U.S. 135 (1950); *United States v. Johnson*, 481 U.S. 681 (1987).

[57] *Patterson v. McLean Credit Union*, 491 U.S. 164 (1989).

[58] *Rust v. Sullivan*, 111 S. Ct. 1759 (1991).

As we shall see in considering many cases cited in this chapter, judges clearly "make law" in construing statutes.[59] Sometimes the statutory language states or implies that the legislature has invited the courts to interpolate particular meaning into the statute.[60] More often, the courts' role arises from the generality of statutory language, as contrasted to the specificity of the fact pattern in any case which raises interpretation. These circumstances may not have been foreseeable by the legislature. The ambiguity discerned in the statute *as applied* then requires a resolution which often was not contemplated by the enacting legislature. In this sense the courts make law in construing legislation, but they do so under the constraint and limitation of the statutory language. Thus, in a difficult case, there may be a lurking question whether a court identified the legislative will, or invented a law of its own. This in turn may raise the perennial and overriding question whether the court, the "non-majoritarian" branch, has overreached.

Those who, like most courts, seek the intent of the enacting legislature, have been described as textualists (including plain meaning advocates) or intentionalists. The textualist's analysis emphasizes the literal words; the intentionalist pursues all objective indicators of the enacting legislature's intent. Some writers have urged that neither textualists nor intentionalists present a convincing case. The two schools are lumped together and labelled "positivistic." Presumably the "deficits" of positivism are that it subscribes to legislative supremacy and the search for the enacting legislature's will. However, we know that these are basic and fiercely held principles, and it is futile to propose that they may be sacrificed in the interest of obtaining a generally accepted methodology for the interpretation of statutes. Nevertheless, we shall recount several such proposals ("equity," "present-orientation," and "legislative purpose") in the following pages.

In 1958 it was said that "American courts have no intelligible, generally accepted and consistently applied theory of statutory interpreta-

---

[59] Scholars of many generations have emphasized the great power the courts implement in their function of statutory interpretation. In point is the anecdote about W. Klem, a famous baseball umpire. After a pitch was thrown, the batter called out "Ball!," and the catcher at the same time yelled, "Strike!," and Klem said, "Gentlemen, it is nothing until I say so."

[60] See *Commonwealth* v. *Cass*, 392 Mass. 799, 801-810 (1984); *Zerofski's Case*, 385 Mass. 590, 594-595 (1982); *Irwin* v. *Ware*, 392 Mass. 745, 752-763 (1984); *Kelly's Case*, 394 Mass. 684 (1985); *Commonwealth* v. *Appleby*, 380 Mass. 296, 303-312 (1980); *Malone* v. *Commonwealth*, 378 Mass. 74 (1979). For examples of such statutes in the federal law, see n.4-9 in Chapter One, *supra*.

tion."[61] There is arguable truth to that statement today, even though, since 1958, tens of thousands of cases, and thousands of pages written by scholars, have concerned statutory interpretation.[62] The approach in this chapter is to emphasize the methodologies that, in the author's opinion, are more frequently used by the courts, and to show some of the divergent views expressed in the cases and scholarly writings.[63]

2. Blackstone's Rules for Statutory Construction

More than two centuries ago, Blackstone set out rules for statutory construction, many of which are observed today:[64]

"The fairest and most rational method to interpret the will of the legislator, is by exploring his intentions at the time when the law was made, by *signs* the most natural and probable. And these signs are either the words, the context, the subject matter, the effects and consequence, or the spirit and reason of the law. Let us take a short view of them all.

"1. Words are generally to be understood in their usual and most known signification; not so much regarding the propriety of grammar, as their general and popular use. Thus the law mentioned by Puffendorf, which forbad a layman to *lay hands* on a priest, was adjudged to extend to him, who had hurt a priest with a weapon. Again; terms of art, or technical terms, must be taken according to the acceptation of the learned in each art, trade, and science. So in the act of settlement, where the crown of England is limited 'to the Princess Sophia, and the heirs of her body, being protestants,' it becomes necessary to call in the assistance of lawyers, to ascertain the precise idea of the words '*heirs of her body*;' which in a legal sense comprise only certain of her lineal descendants. Lastly, where words are clearly repugnant in two laws, the later law takes place of the elder: *leges priores contrarias abrogant* is a maxim of universal law, as well as of our own

---

[61] Hart and Sacks, "The Legal Process; Basic Problems in the Making and Application of Law," 1201 (tent. ed., Cambridge, 1958).

[62] See generally, Eskridge and Frickey, "Cases and Materials on Legislation; Statutes and the Creation of Public Policy," 569-828 (1988).

[63] It is not uncommon to find that there is sometimes inconsistency in methodology from case to case in the same court. As to the scholarly writings, it is probably true that many judges do not read them.

[64] 1 Blackstone's Commentaries 59-62 (8th ed. 1778)

constitutions. And accordingly it was laid down by a law of the twelve tables at Rome, *quod populus postremum iussit, id ius ratum esto.*

"2. If words happen to be still dubious, we may establish their meaning from the *context*; with which it may be of singular use to compare a word, or a sentence, whenever they are ambiguous, equivocal, or intricate. Thus the proeme, or preamble, is often called in to help the construction of an act of parliament. Of the same nature and use is the comparison of a law with other laws, that are made by the same legislator, that have some affinity with the subject, or that expressly relate to the same point. Thus, when the law of England declares murder to be felony without benefit of clergy, we must resort to the same law of England to learn what the benefit of clergy is: and when the common law censures simoniacal contracts, it affords great light to the subject to consider what the canon law has adjudged to be simony.

"3. As to the *subject matter*, words are always to be understood as having a regard thereto; for that is always supposed to be in the eye of the legislator, and all his expressions directed to that end. Thus, when a law of our Edward III forbids all ecclesiastical persons to purchase *provisions* at Rome, it might seem to prohibit the buying of grain and other victual; but when we consider that the statute was made to repress the usurpations of the papal fee, and that the nominations to benefices by the pope were called provisions, we shall see that the restraint is intended to be laid upon such provisions only.

"4. As to the *effects* and *consequence*, the rule is, that where words bear either none, or a very absurd signification, if literally understood, we must a little deviate from the received sense of them. Therefore the Belognian law, mentioned by Puffendorf, which enacted 'that whoever drew blood in the streets should be punished with the utmost severity,' was held after long debate not to extend to the surgeon, who opened the vein of a person that fell down in the street with a fit.

"5. But, lastly, the most universal and effectual way of discovering the true meaning of a law, when the words are dubious, is by considering the *reason* and *spirit* of it; or the cause which moved the legislator to enact it. For when this reason ceases, the law itself ought likewise to cease with it. An instance of this is given in a case put by Cicero, or whoever was the author of the rhetorical treatise inscribed to Herennius. There was a law, that those who in a storm forsook the ship should forfeit all property therein; and the ship and lading should belong entirely to those who staid in it. In a dangerous tempest all the mariners forsook the ship, except only one sick passenger, who by reason of his disease was unable to get out and escape. By chance the ship came safe to port. The sick man kept possession, and claimed the benefit of the law. Now here all the learned agree, that the sick man is not within the reason of the law; for the reason of making it was to give encouragement to such as should venture their lives to save the vessel: but this is a merit, which he could never pretend to, who neither staid in the ship upon that account, nor contributed anything to its preservation.

"From this method of interpreting laws, by reason of them, arises what we call *equity*; which is thus defined by Grotius, 'the correction of that, wherein the law (by reason of its universality) is deficient.' For since in laws all cases cannot be foreseen or expressed, it is necessary, that when the general decrees of the law come to be applied to particular cases, there should be somewhere a power vested of defining those circumstances, which (had they been foreseen) the legislator himself would have expressed. And these are the cases, which according to Grotius, '*lex non exacte definite, sed arbitrio boni viri permittit.*'

"Equity thus depending, essentially, upon the particular circumstances of each individual case, there can be no established rules and fixed precepts of equity laid down, without destroying its very essence, and reducing it to a positive law. And, on the other hand, the liberty of considering all cases in a equitable light must not be indulged too far, lest thereby we destroy all law, and leave the decision of every question entirely in the breast of the judge. And law, without equity, though hard and disagreeable, is much more desirable for the public good, than equity without law: which would make every judge a legislator, and introduce most infinite confusion; as there would then be almost as many different rules of action laid down in our courts, as there are differences of capacity and sentiment in the human mind."

3. Three Controversial Concepts: "Equity," "Present-Orientation," and "Legislative Purpose" Theories

Concepts of "equity," "present-orientation" or "legislative purpose" can lead to spurious results in construing a statute, because these concepts are not aimed at discovering the intent of the enacting legislature.

Some early cases stated that the meaning of a statute could be varied in order to do "equity" (or justice) to the parties.[65] There is a temptation to distort the fair meaning of the statutory language to avoid what the court believes is an inequitable effect upon a litigant. This contradicts the premise that avoidance of unjust results, without more, should not control the court's interpretation. "Nor does it matter in such a situation whether the consequences in a given case are unjust or inequitable, if they are not absurd."[66] It has been submitted that the equity doctrine may be brought within the realm of valid interpretation, as now understood, only if the doctrine is confined to making a choice from two or more possible meanings that the statutory words will bear by fair use of language, after all normal techniques for making such a choice have failed to give a solution.[67]

Similarly, spurious results may ensue if the court follows the course of "present-orientation." The search for legislative intent has been traditionally an historical exercise. The court must relate to the legislature which passed the statute, and the circumstances which then existed. Nevertheless, some scholars have urged that interpretation should be oriented to the present, and results should equate with contemporary needs and values.[68] This approach has appeal because of the difficulty of recreating the original legislative intent, and because justice may be well served, perhaps best served, by the court's judgment.

---

[65] See many cases cited, almost all from antiquity, in deSloovere, "The Equity and the Reason of a Statute," 21 Cornell L.Q. 591 (1936). See n.102 and n.104, *infra*, for cites to several cases which, at first blush, appear to be decided solely on the equity concept but, on further analysis it appears that the court in each case applied generally accepted methodology.

[66] *Id*. at 612.

[67] *Id*. at 609.

[68] Dworkin, "Law's Empire," 313-354 (1986); Aleinikoff, "Updating Statutory Interpretation," 87 Mich. L. Rev. 20 (1988); Calabresi, "A Common Law for the Age of Statutes" (1982).

Proponents of present-orientation emphasize the shortcomings of both the "plain meaning" and "intent" rules as limiting the competence of both legislature and courts as law-makers. An argument for present-orientation is that it makes the statute the best that it can be. The premise is that the legislature establishes a policy and the court implements that policy; and thus the law can grow, example by example, like the common law, because the court "would be authorized to nurture statutory principles in ways that would transcend a view of [the legislative] intent confined to the instant of enactment."[69]

Present-orientation has not ordinarily been the approach of the courts, state or federal, and some scholars have rightly rejected the thesis on the ground that a court which consciously invokes present-orientation is engaged in an impermissible exercise.[70] Present-orientation is a departure from traditional concepts of separation of powers. The statute which is detached from its original source and circumstances is a nothing, and the judicial construction is an invention of the court. Under the constitutions, the legislatures are the supreme law-makers, and the courts may not, under the guise of interpretation, usurp "a power which our democracy has lodged in its elected legislature."[71]

There is no question that in some difficult cases there is a danger that courts may unintentionally apply present-orientation. There is a well established concept that a statute may be construed to recognize future events which the legislature could not have predicted. Restrained thinking by the court may be required to avoid present-oriented value judgments.[72]

The pursuit of "legislative purpose" is also misguided. On speaking here of legislative purpose we do not refer to the use by some courts of that term as a synonym for the general intent of the enacting legisla-

---

[69] Note, "Intent, Clear Statements and the Common Law: Statutory Interpretation in the Supreme Court," 95 Harv. L. Rev. 892, 914 (1982).

[70] See, e.g., Smith, "Law Without Mind," 88 Mich. L. Rev. 104 (1989). The title is apt, to indicate the author's emphatic rejection of present-orientation.

[71] Frankfurter, "Some Reflections on the Reading of Statutes," 47 Colum. L. Rev. 527, 533 (1947).

[72] See, e.g., *Commonwealth* v. *Welosky*, 276 Mass. 398, 407-411 (1931), wherein by statute jurors were drawn from voting lists; women were not eligible to vote when the statute was enacted. Subsequently the Nineteenth Amendment was passed, and women were voters. Held, women did not thereby become eligible as jurors under the voting lists statute.

ture.[73] However, an approach which elects "legislative purpose" as a *substitute* for legislative intent may lead to erroneous results. The premise is that the enacting legislature had a general aim or purpose, and that is what the courts should seek rather than the enacting legislature's intent. The theory pursues the will of the legislature in a general sense, but extends liberality to the court's function of interpretation. Thus in 1958, Professors Hart and Sacks wrote: "The function of a court interpreting a statute is to decide what meaning *ought* to be given to the direction of the statute in respects relevant to the case before it.... This does not mean to say that the court's function is to ascertain the intention of the legislature with respect to the matter in issue" (emphasis supplied).[74]

The "purpose" concept apparently enjoyed a limited period of credibility, but then suffered a decline as emphasis returned to legislative intent, and even literalism, in construing statutes.[75]

In sum, scholars have responded variously to the continuing uncertainty and controversy in the courts' approach to statutory interpretation. Some would abandon the pursuit of the enacting legislature's intent, and would substitute something akin to a common law exercise by the courts. Certainly, consideration of the aim or purpose of the legislature, or equitable considerations (i.e., the legislature did not intend to be unjust), are valid circumstances to be weighed with other factors in construing legislative intent. They are not valid circumstances if they are projected as *substitutes* for legislative intent. Such an approach would

---

[73] See *United Steelworkers* v. *Weber*, 443 U.S. 193 (1979), where the court relied on legislative history in interpreting the statute, but also said that its reasoning reflected the "spirit" of the statute. See also *Van Beck* v. *Sabine*, 300 U.S. 342, 351 (1937).

[74] Hart and Sacks, "The Legal Process: Basic Problems in the Making and Application of Law," 1410 (tent. ed. Cambridge 1958). The authors go on to say, at 1411, "In interpreting a statute a court should:

"1. Decide what purpose ought to be attributed to the statute and to any subordinate provision of it which may be involved; and then

"2. Interpret the words of the statute immediately in question so as to carry out the purpose as best it can, making sure, however, that it does not give the words either - (a) a meaning they will not bear, or (b) a meaning which would violate any established policy of clear statement."

[75] See Note, *supra* note 68, at 892. The authors at 893 identify three cases which look to "purpose": *J.T. Case Co.*, v. *Borak*, 377 U.S. 426, 433 (1964); *Bingler* v. *Johnson*, 394 U.S. 741, 751-752 (1969); *Moragne* v. *States Marine Lines, Inc.*, 398 U.S. 375, 392 (1970). Thereafter the authors trace the emphatic decline of the concept of legislative purpose.

require a considerable recasting of familiar and accepted principles of separation of powers and the supremacy of the legislatures as lawmakers.

4. Legislative Intent: Plain Meaning

The plain meaning rule states that when the language of a statute is plain and does not lead, in the case before the court, to absurd or impracticable results, there is no occasion or excuse for judicial construction; the language must then be accepted by the courts as the sole evidence of the ultimate legislative intent, and the courts have no function but to apply and enforce the statute accordingly.[76] Stated another way: when the language is plain and admits of no more than one meaning, the duty of interpretation does not arise and the rules which are to aid doubtful meaning need no discussion.[77]

The plain meaning rule has often been rejected as unhelpful,[78] but the rule continues to have strong supporters.[79] A hope has been expressed that the rule is extinct,[80] but nevertheless it has been decisive in some recent cases.[81] It is also true that there is sustenance for the spirit of plain meaning when the courts balance the statutory words heavily against other circumstances, especially legislative history.[82] The major premise opposing the plain meaning approach is that the inquiry in every case should be for the enacting legislature's "intent," and that

---

[76] *Caminetti* v. *United States*, 242 U.S. 470, 485 (1917).

[77] See *Hamilton* v. *Rathbone*, 175 U.S. 414, 421 (1899); *Hashimi* v. *Kalil*, 388 Mass. 607, 609 (1983).

[78] See, e.g., *United States* v. *American Trucking Ass'ns*, 310 U.S. 534, 543-544 (1960); *Cass* v. *United States*, 417 U.S. 72, 76-79 (1974).

[79] "Where it is clear that the unambiguous language of a statute embraces certain conduct, and it would not be patently absurd to apply the statute to such conduct, it does not foster a democratic exegesis for this Court to rummage through unauthoritative materials to consult the spirit of the legislation in order to discover an alternative interpretation of the statute with which the Court is more comfortable." *Public Citizen* v. *United States Dept. of Justice*, 491 U.S. 440, 473 (1989) (Kennedy, J., concurring in judgment).

"[I]t must be assumed that what the Members of the House and Senators thought they were voting for, and what the President thought he was approving when he signed the bill, was what the text plainly said, rather than what a few Representatives, or even a committee report said it said." *United States* v. *Taylor*, 487 U.S. 326, 345 (1988) (Scalia, J., concurring in part).

[80] Kernochan, "Statutory Interpretation: An Outline of Method," 3 Dalhousie L. J. 331, 340-341 (1976-1977).

[81] See cases cited *id.* at 340, note 30.

[82] See, e.g., *United States* v. *Monsanto*, 491 U.S. 600, 606-611 (1989); *Patterson* v. *McLean Credit Union*, 491 U.S. 164, 171-175 (1989).

---

further search beyond the statute's words should not be precluded even where the legislative words are facially unambiguous.[83] The reasoning is that words in many instances are vague in meaning.[84] Frankfurter argues that the plain meaning rule is simplistic; that nothing which is logically relevant should be excluded from consideration.[85] Learned Hand wrote, "There is no surer way to misread any document than to read it literally. . . ."[86] Holmes said that "[a] word is not a crystal, transparent and unchanged, it is the skin of a living thought and may vary greatly in color and content according to the circumstances and the time in which it is used."[87]

5. Legislative Intent: Multiple Indicia

The most common approach of the courts seeks the legislative intent by examining not only the literal language of the statute, but also other relevant objective circumstances, especially legislative history, all in light of the facts of the case which raise the issue of interpretation. Although the court may eschew a plain meaning approach, it is common to find controversy in the relative weight which the court apportions to literalism as opposed to consideration of other objective evidence of legislative intent.

It is useful to distinguish between specific and general intent. Specific intent is narrow in its scope, ordinarily well defined by the literal lan-

---

[83]The apparent deemphasis on literalism is not intended to denigrate the primary importance of the legislative language. It is said that Felix Frankfurter, who clearly was no advocate of the plain meaning rule, exhorted his students to "(1) read the statute; (2) read the statute; (3) read the statute." H. Friendly, "Benchmarks" 202 (1967). A court which concludes that there is no ambiguity in the statute, and notes in some form of words the "plain" or "clear" meaning of the statute, but *also* examines the extraneous circumstances as supportive of the result, is not applying the plain meaning rule. Rather, it is emphasizing the primary importance of the statutory words in the search for legislative intent.

[84]The emphasis here is on "in many instances," because of course there are instances where the statute's words in their context permit only one meaning, however closely extraneous factors are scrutinized for objective evidence supportive of a second meaning. See the dialogue set forth in Easterbrook, "Legal Interpretation and the Power of the Judiciary," 7 Harv. J.L. & Pub. Pol'y 87 (1984) and Epstein, "The Pitfalls of Interpretation," 7 Harv. J.L. & Pub. Pol'y 101 (1984).

[85] Frankfurter, "Some Reflections on the Reading of Statutes," 47 Colum. L. Rev. 527, 541 (1947) ("These current English rules of construction are simple. They are too simple. If the purpose of construction is the ascertainment of meaning, nothing that is logically relevant should be excluded.")

[86]*Guiseppi v. Walling*, 144 F.2d 608, 624 (2d Cir. 1944) (Hand, J., concurring).

[87]*Towne v. Eisner*, 245 U.S. 418, 425 (1918).

guage of the statute, and relates to the immediate legislative concern at the time of enactment. Where the language of the statute is ambiguous as applied to the facts at issue, the specific intent may not be helpful.

The search for a general legislative intent may involve many avenues, and all of these should be explored in light of the facts of the case before the court. Courts frequently rely for decision upon a combination of two or more indicia. The search must begin with the words of the statute as the primary source. If the contested provision is part of a larger statute, or if there are surrounding or related statutes, appraisal is made in light of the context. Title, preamble and declarations of purpose are considered. Legislative history of the statute prior to its enactment is reviewed as well as other evidence of circumstances (e.g., social and economic) which may be relevant to the enactment. The relevance of certain postenactment developments may be argued. Various maxims, canons or rules of construction may be applied by the court.

We turn in ensuing sections to a discussion of the several indicia of legislative intent.

6. Legislative History

Where the search for intent turns to sources other than the words, the principal recourse is to the history of the statute's enactment. Examination turns to the history of amendments and proposed amendments to the statute at issue,[88] and other statutes related in substance and in time of enactment.[89] More often, reliance is placed on legislative committee reports, or on statements of legislators in floor debate. Such background material is ordinarily available in greater quantity and detail in the Congress than in the state legislatures.

Not surprisingly, emphatic differences of opinion, as to the importance and value of legislative history, have been expressed by the Justices of the Supreme Court. It has been opined that recourse should be had to no more than committee reports.[90] Other justices have in effect urged in some cases that legislative history be disregarded and that the plain

---

[88] See *Aldoupolis* v. *Commonwealth*, 386 Mass. 260, 264-265 (1982).

[89] See *Commonwealth* v. *Sefranka*, 382 Mass. 108, 112-116 (1980).

[90] *Schwegmann Bros.* v. *Calvert Corp.*, 341 U.S. 384, 395-396 (1951) (Jackson, J., concurring).

meaning principle be applied.[91] In other cases a majority of the court has de-emphasized the importance of legislative history.[92]

Post-enactment action (or inaction) by Congress or a state legislature has been argued as determinative especially in cases where the court is urged to overrule or modify its prior interpretation of a statute. Legislative silence after a decision of the court is ordinarily not to be taken as legislative approval of the court's prior rulings of law.[93] "It is at best treacherous to find in congressional silence alone the adoption of a controlling rule of law."[94] Among other considerations is the fact, in most cases, that the "silent" legislature is not the enacting legislature, but a different body. Where a court declined to adopt a "discovery rule" for determining when a cause of action accrued, and the legislature subsequently failed to pass a bill proposing a discovery rule, the court thereafter declined to view the legislative inaction as a disapproval of a discovery rule or an acceptance of the court's prior holding.[95] "The fallacy in [an argument that defeat of a bill in the legislature is significant] is that no one knows why the legislature did not pass the propose measures. . . . The practicalities of the legislative process furnish many reasons for the lack of success of a measure other than legislative dislike for the principle involved in the legislation."[96]

"It is a general principle of statutory construction that the reenact-

---

[91] See *Public Citizen* v. *United States Dept. of Justice*, 491 U.S. 440, 473 (1989) (Kennedy, J., concurring in judgment); *United States* v. *Taylor*, 487 U.S. 326, 345 (1988) (Scalia, J., concurring in part).

[92] *United States* v. *Monsanto*, 491 U.S. at 606-611 (1989); *Patterson* v. *McLean Credit Union*, 491 U.S. at 171-175 (1989). Compare *United Steelworkers* v. *Weber*, 443 U.S. at 193 (1979), where both the majority and dissenters of a divided court relied upon extensive quotations from various legislators in floor debates.

[93] *Boys Markets, Inc.* v. *Retail Clerks Union, Local 770*, 398 U.S. 235, 242 (1970). But see *Flood* v. *Kuhn*, 407 U.S. 258, 269-285 (1972), where a divided court held that the long-standing exemption of professional baseball from the antitrust laws is an established aberration, in light of the court's holding that other interstate professional sports are not similarly exempt, but one in which Congress by silence has acquiesced, and that is entitled to the benefit of stare decisis. The court opined that removal of the resultant inconsistency at this late date is a matter for legislative, not judicial, resolution.

[94] *Girouard* v. *United States*, 328 U.S. 61, 69 (1946).

[95] *Franklin* v. *Albert*, 381 Mass. 611, 615-617 (1980).

[96] *Berry* v. *Branner*, 245 Or. 30 , 311 (1966). It is also true that the court seeks the will of the enacting legislature, and the views of subsequent legislatures are not relevant.

ment of a statute in substantially the same words does not change its meaning or extend its scope. Its words are presumed to continue to have attached to them the same sense as in the preceding enactment."[97]

Post-enactment comments of individual legislators "form a hazardous basis" for an argument as to legislative intent.[98]

7. Stare Decisis

Important policy considerations militate in favor of continuity and predictability in the law.[99] The burden borne by the party advocating the abandonment of an established precedent is especially great where a court is asked to overrule a point of statutory construction. The principle of stare decisis has special force in the area of statutory interpretation, for here, unlike cases concerning constitutional law, the legislature remains free to alter what the court has done.[100] "Having given our view on the meaning of a statute, our task is concluded, absent extraordinary circumstances. When the Court changes its mind years later, simply because the judges have changed, in my judgment it takes upon itself the function of the legislature."[101] However, precedents are not sacrosanct. "Stare decisis certainly does not require a court to perpetuate a wrong for which it was responsible, especially when no rights have accrued in reliance of the error."[102] The court may overrule a prior

---

[97] *Commonwealth* v. *Welosky*, 276 Mass. 398, 409 (1931). See *Buck Stove & Range Co.* v. *Vickers*, 226 U.S. 205, 213 (1912).

[98] *United States* v. *Monsanto*, 491 U.S. at 610 (1989).

[99] Compare the discussion of stare decisis in Chapter Two, The Common Law, *supra*.

[100] *Patterson* v. *McLean Credit Union*, 491 U.S. 164, 172-173 (1989).

[101] *Boys Markets, Inc.* v. *Retail Clerks Union, Local 770*, 398 U.S. at 258 (Black, J., dissenting).

[102] *Cleveland* v. *United States*, 329 U.S. 14, 28 (1946) (Murphy, J., dissenting). The *Cleveland* case is one in a line of cases concerning the Mann Act, extending over several decades, wherein the Supreme Court struggled with the tension between the principle of stare decisis and the strong argument that the Mann Act (the "White Slave Act") was erroneously construed by the court in its first consideration of the statute (*Caminetti* v. *United States*, 242 U.S. 470, 485-486 [1917]) where it said that interstate transportation of women in interstate commerce for "prostitution or debauchery, or for any other immoral purpose" violated the law although there was no showing of pecuniary gain as a motive. See the analysis of the statute and these cases in Levi, "An Introduction to Legal Reasoning," 33-57 (1949).

See *United States* v. *Johnson*, 481 U.S. 681, 692-703 (1987), wherein four justices dissented from the court's perpetuating and extending the rule of *Feres* v. *United States*, 340 U.S. 135 (1950), which excluded the claims of certain servicemen under the Federal Tort Claims Act, although "... Congress not only failed to provide such an exemption, but quite plainly excluded it." *Id.* at 692 (Scalia, J., dissenting).

---

statutory construction based on further action taken by the legislature,[103] or growth in judicial doctrine, as viewed in light of new fact patterns raised in cases which put the prior interpretation at issue.[104]

8. Saving a Statute's Constitutionality

It is an elementary rule that every reasonable construction must be resorted to in order to save a statute from unconstitutionality.[105] Thus, as between two possible interpretations of a statute, by one of which it would be unconstitutional and by the other valid, the court's plain duty is to adopt that which will save the act.[106] Further, a statute must be construed, if fairly possible, so as to avoid not only the conclusion that it is unconstitutional, but grave doubts upon that score.[107] Courts have even modified (some would say "rewritten") statutory language, to avoid constitutional challenge.[108]

9. Deference to Interpretation by Agency

In instances requiring interpretation of a statute administered by an agency it has been customary to afford deference to the agency's interpretation of the authorizing statute.[109] The agency's interpretation may be shown by its regulations[110] or by its decisions in particular cases.[111] If a statute is "silent or ambiguous with respect to the specific issue, the question for the court is whether the agency's answer is based on a permissible construction of the statute."[112]

---

[103] *Franklin* v. *Albert*, 381 Mass. 611, 614-615 (1980).

[104] *Commonwealth* v. *Maguire*, 392 Mass. 466, 468-470 (1984), wherein the court overruled a statutory interpretation based in part on the results and reasoning of relevant cases in other jurisdictions.

[105] *Rust* v. *Sullivan*, 111 S. Ct. 1759, 1771 (1991) and cases cited. *NLRB* v. *Catholic Bishop of Chicago*, 440 U.S. 490, 500 (1979); *Beeler* v. *Downey*, 387 Mass. 609, 613-615 (1982); *Commonwealth* v. *Joyce*, 382 Mass. 222, 226 n.5 (1981).

[106] *Blodgett* v. *Holden*, 275 U.S. 142, 148 (1927).

[107] *United States* v. *Jin Fuey Moy*, 241 U.S. 394, 401 (1916) (citation deleted).

[108] *Care and Protection of Charles*, 399 Mass. 324, 333, 337-340 (1987) (guidelines for school departments inserted by court to avoid challenge of unconstitutional delegation by legislature); *Pryor* v. *Municipal Court*, 25 Cal. 3d 238, 244, 256, 257 (1979); *Commonwealth* v. *Sefranka*, 382 Mass. 108, 112-118 (1980) (court limited and modified statutory language to avoid unconstitutional vagueness).

[109] *Rust* v. *Sullivan*, 111 S. Ct. at 1767, citing *Chevron U.S.A. Inc.* v. *Natural Resources Defense Council, Inc.*, 467 U.S. 837, 842-843 (1984).

[110] *Id.*

[111] *Kelly's Case*, 394 Mass. 684, 690 (1985) (Hennessey, C.J., dissenting).

[112] *Rust* v. *Sullivan*, 111 S. Ct. at 1767, citing *Chevron U.S.A. Inc.* v. *Natural Resources Defense Council, Inc.*, 467 U.S. 837, 842-843 (1984).

"The [agency's] construction of [the statute] may not be disturbed as an abuse of discretion if it reflects a plausible construction of the plain language of the statute and does not otherwise conflict with Congress' expressed intent."[113] In deferring to the expertise of the agency in the interpretation, the court need not conclude that the agency construction was the only permissible one, or even the reading that the court would have reached if the question initially had arisen in a judicial proceeding.[114] The court may defer to the agency's views even when it is shown that those views are inconsistent with the agency's prior construction of the statute, especially when the agency has demonstrated circumstances which explain its changed position.[115]

Particular deference has been given to an agency's interpretation where the statute itself vests broad powers in the agency to fill in the details of the legislative scheme.[116]

10. Maxims, Canons, Presumptions and Rules of Construction

Rules of construction, by whatever name they are called, have been denigrated as a mechanical and unhelpful approach to statutory interpretation.[117] They have been named as judicial contrivances to support otherwise unsupported results.[118] Perhaps the criticism is overblown, because some of the rules as applied comport with common sense[119]

---

[113]*Id.*

[114]*Chevron U.S.A. Inc.* v. *Natural Resources Defense Council, Inc.*, 467 U.S. at 843, n.11 (1984).

[115]*Motor Vehicle Mfrs. Ass'n of U.S.* v. *State Farm Mut. Auto. Ins. Co.*, 463 U.S. 29, 42 (1983). *Rust* v. *Sullivan*, 111 S. Ct. at 1769, and cases cited.

[116]*Amherst-Pelham Regional Sch. Comm.* v. *Department of Educ.*, 376 Mass. 480, 492 (1978).

[117]See, e.g., Posner, "Statutory Interpretation in the Classroom and in the Courtroom," 50 U. Chi. L. Rev. 800, 806 (1983). Judge Posner analyzes and rejects (as "plain wrong") many canons as not reflective of legislative reasoning. He also rejects the premise that legislators and their staffs are aware of the canons.

[118]See Llewellyn's famous put-down of canons of construction in "Remarks on Theory of Appellate Decision," 3 Vand. L. Rev. 395, 401-406 (1950) wherein the author presents 28 such canons ("thrusts") and 28 others ("parrys") of opposed meaning.

[119]See, e.g., *Caminetti* v. *United States* and *Cleveland* v. *United States, supra*, note 102, in this chapter, for the proposition that a rational and early application of the canon ejusdem generis (see it defined in section 11, and *post*) might have avoided several decades of litigation, and a number of incarcerations. But see the comment of Radin, "Statutory Interpretation," 43 Harv. L. Rev. 863, 873, 874 (1930), that the canon

and, moreover, probably some of them are known to both legislation drafters and courts and thus provide some basis for a common understanding of the meaning of statutory words and phrases. In any event, and most importantly, courts continue to rely on rules of construction, usually in conjunction with other indicia of legislative intent.

In preceding sections we have already alluded to several rules of construction (the plain meaning rule; deference to agency interpretation; saving a statute's constitutionality) and in the following section we list a number of rules commonly used by the courts.

11. Some Examples of Rules of Construction

The words of the statute are the main source for the ascertainment of a legislative purpose.[120]

Statutory words are presumed, unless the contrary appears, to be used in their ordinary sense, with the meaning commonly attributed to them.[121]

Words that bear a specific meaning to a class in the community (technical, legal, professional or commercial) are construed the way that class would, unless the court believes that the legislature intended that the general meaning apply, or if the specialized meaning is contrary to the implications of context or the subject-matter.[122]

General expressions may be restrained by relevant circumstances showing a legislative intent that they be narrowed and used in a particular sense.[123]

When an act provides that it shall be known and referred to by a designated name, the name cannot be made the means of overriding the plain meaning of its other provisions.[124]

---

ejusdem generis is "a direct contradiction to the habit of speech of most persons."

See also Finkelstein, "In Re Brett: The Sticky Problem of Statutory Construction," 52 Fordham L. Rev. 430 (1983), wherein the author makes witty, but also adroit, use of canons in analyzing the application of the official baseball rules to the famous case involving player George Brett who allegedly violated the rule against excessive use of pine tar on his bat.

[120]*Commonwealth* v. *Welosky*, 276 Mass. 398, 401 (1931).

[121]*Hashimi* v. *Kalil*, 388 Mass. 607, 609 (1983); *Commonwealth* v. *Maguire*, 392 Mass. 466, 470 (1984); *Commonwealth* v. *Welosky*, 276 Mass. 398, 401 (1931).

[122]See Sutherland Stat. Constr. § 47.27 (4th ed., 1984). See also *Simon* v. *State Examiners of Electricians*, 395 Mass. 238, 242-249 (1985) (O'Connor, J., joined by Hennessey, C.J., dissenting).

[123]*Duggan* v. *Bay State St. Rwy.*, 230 Mass. 370, 374 (1918).

[124]*Caminetti* v. *United States*, 242 U.S. 470, 489-490 (1917).

Where two statutes are inconsistent and mutually repugnant, the later statute governs.[125]

Statutes should be read so as to give effect to all parts of the legislation; no part of the legislation is to be treated as surplusage.[126]

The court must decide what part of the preamble the legislature intended as its definition of the statute's words.[127]

A thing may be within the letter of the statute and yet not within the statute, because not within its spirit, nor within the intention of its makers, and, thus, a statute must be read against the background of the legislative history of an Act and the historical context from which the Act arose.[128]

Statutes are to be interpreted, not alone according to their simple, literal or strict verbal meaning, but in connection with their development, their progression through the legislative body, the history of the times, and prior legislation.[129]

The court in construing a statute may properly look for meaning in a pattern of related statutes.[130]

It is at best treacherous to find in congressional silence alone the adoption of a controlling rule of law.[131] The consideration and rejection by the legislature of various proposed measures since the court last construed the statute should not control the court's decision in reconsidering the statute.[132]

In the absence of any persuasive circumstances evidencing a clear design that congressional inaction be taken as acceptance of a decision of the court, the mere silence of the legislature is not a sufficient reason for refusing to reconsider the decision.[133]

It is a general principle of statutory construction that the reenactment of a statute in substantially the same words does not change its meaning or extend its scope. Its words are presumed to continue to have attached

---

[125] *Mirageas* v. *Massachusetts Bay Transp. Auth.*, 391 Mass. 815, 819 (1984).

[126] *Noble* v. *Marshall*, 650 F.2d 1058, 1061 (9th Cir., 1981).

[127] *Commonwealth* v. *Thorpe*, 384 Mass. 271, 276-277 (1981).

[128] *United Steelworkers* v. *Weber*, 443 U.S. at 201 (1979).

[129] *Commonwealth* v. *Welosky*, 276 Mass. 398, 401 (1931).

[130] *Van Beeck* v. *Sabine Towing Co.*, 300 U.S. 342, 351 (1937).

[131] *Girouard* v. *United States*, 328 U.S. at 69.

[132] *Franklin* v. *Albert*, 381 Mass. 611, 615-616 (1980).

[133] *Helvering* v. *Hallock*, 309 U.S. 106, 119-122 (1940).

to them the same sense as in the preceding enactment.[134]

Stare decisis is usually the wise policy, because in most matters it is more important that the applicable rule of law be settled than that it be settled right.[135]

The burden borne by the party advocating the abandonment of an established precedent is greater where the Court is asked to overrule a point of statutory construction. Considerations of stare decisis have special force in the area of statutory interpretation, for here, unlike in the context of constitutional interpretation, the legislative power is implicated, and Congress remains free to alter what the court has done.[136]

Courts should construe statutes to avoid decision as to their constitutionality;[137] when there is a valid alternative ground for relief, the appellate court need not reach the constitutional contentions of the parties.[138]

The court's conclusion that a penal statute is unconstitutionally vague as construed by past decisions does not require the court to invalidate the provision; if a reasonable narrowing construction to a vague statute can be supplied, this court may do so in order to sustain the statute's constitutional validity.[139]

Statutes framed in general terms commonly look to the future and may include conditions as they arise from time to time not even known at the time of enactment, provided they are fairly within the sweep and the meaning of the words and falling within their obvious scope and purpose. But statutes do not govern situations not within the reason of their enactment and spawned by circumstances wholly outside of the dominating purpose of those who framed and enacted them.[140]

---

[134]*Commonwealth* v. *Welosky*, 276 Mass. 398, 409 (1931). *See* v. *Building Comm'r of Springfield*, 246 Mass. 340, 343 (1923) (revision read in light of preexisting statutes and as a continuation of earlier provisions unless a clear indication of intent to change meaning).

[135]*Burnet* v. *Coronado Oil & Gas Co.*, 285 U.S. 393, 406 (1932) (Brandeis, J., dissenting).

[136]*Patterson* v. *McLean Credit Union*, 491 U.S. at 172-173, and cases cited.

[137]*Beeler* v. *Downey*, 387 Mass. 609, 613 (1982).

[138]*Rust* v. *Sullivan*, 111 S. Ct. at 1778-1780 (1991) (Blackmun, J., dissenting); *International Ass'n of Machinists* v. *Street*, 367 U.S. 740, 749 (1961).

[139]*Commonwealth* v. *Sefranka*, 382 Mass. 108, 115-116 (1980); *Commonwealth* v. *Joyce*, 382 Mass. 222, 226 n.5, 232-233 (1981).

[140]*Wolfe* v. *Ford Motor Co.*, 386 Mass. 95, 99 (1982); *Hayon* v. *Coca Cola Bottling Co. of N.E.*, 375 Mass. 644, 649 (1978); *Commonwealth* v. *Welosky*, 276 Mass. 398, 403 (1931).

The legislature may intentionally and clearly leave the construction of the statute's words to the courts.[141]

The legislature must be presumed to have known the meaning which the court in construing a statute had attributed to particular words when the legislature subsequently employed the same words in a similar association in an analogous statute.[142]

A state court, in construing its own state statute, is not bound by, although may find guidance from, interpretations of an analogous federal statute.[143]

Where the legislature has employed specific language in one paragraph, but not in another, the language should not be implied where it is not present.[144]

Where words are used in one part of a statute in a definite sense, they should be given the same meaning in another part of the statute.[145]

Civil rights statutes are entitled to liberal construction.[146]

Remedial statutes are entitled to liberal construction. Cases within the reason, although not within the letter, of a remedial statute are embraced by its provisions.[147]

There is a presumption against a legislative intention to change existing law; thus statutes in derogation of the common law are to be strictly construed.[148]

The court must resolve in favor of criminal defendants any reasonable doubt as to the statute's meaning.[149]

Ordinary rules of statutory construction require the court to construe any criminal statute strictly against the government.[150]

---

[141]*Irwin* v. *Ware*, 392 Mass. 745, 752-753 (1984); *Commonwealth* v. *Cass*, 392 Mass. 799, 801 (1984). See *Commonwealth* v. *Appleby*, 380 Mass. 296, 303 (1980), and *Malone* v. *Commonwealth*, 378 Mass. 74, 77 (1979).

[142]*Commonwealth* v. *Cass*, 392 Mass. 799, 801 (1984). *MacQuarrie* v. *Balch*, 362 Mass. 151, 152 (1972).

[143]*College-Town* v. *Massachusetts Comm. Against Discrimination*, 400 Mass. 156, 163 (1987).

[144]*Beeler* v. *Downey*, 387 Mass. 609, 616 (1982).

[145]*Plymouth County Nuclear Information Comm., Inc.* v. *Energy Facilities Siting Council*, 374 Mass. 236, 240 (1978).

[146]*Redgrave* v. *Boston Symphony Orchestra*, 399 Mass. 93, 99 (1987); *Batchelder* v. *Allied Stores Corp.*, 393 Mass. 819, 821-822 (1985).

[147]*O'Connell* v. *Chasdi*, 400 Mass. 686, 694 (1987).

[148]*Johnson* v. *Southern Pacific Co.*, 196 U.S. 1, 17 (1904).

[149]*Commonwealth* v. *Rhodes*, 389 Mass. 641, 647 (1983).

[150]*Aldoupolis* v. *Commonwealth*, 386 Mass. 260, 264-267 (1928).

Though penal laws are to be construed strictly, yet the intention of the legislature must govern in the construction of penal as well as other statutes; and they are not to be construed so strictly as to defeat the obvious intention of the legislature.[151]

The canon in favor of strict construction of penal statutes is not an inexorable command to override common sense and evident statutory purpose.[152]

There is a strong presumption against implied repeal, and the presumption is overcome only if there is sufficiently clear indication that the legislature intended by its action to repeal its former action.[153]

Even in cases where it is logically possible that the prior statute continue in force as an exception to a more general subsequent statute, courts have held that there was implied repeal where it was necessary to give effect to the apparent legislative intent.[154]

There is a presumption that a statute is constitutional.[155]

The canon noscitur a sociis states that words take meaning from those with which they are associated.[156]

The canon ejusdem generis states that a general term that follows a set of specific terms is to be limited to items of the same general class as contained in the recital of specifics, and cannot be used to enlarge the class; the general words cannot be confined more narrowly than the class of which they are a part.[157]

The canon expressio unis est exclusio alterius states that the expression of some excludes others; those things not enumerated are not implied.[158]

12. Some Further Comments About Enacted Law

When, in 1958, Professors Hart and Sacks accurately opined that American courts have no intelligible, generally accepted and consistently applied theory of statutory interpretation, they proceeded in the obvious

---

[151]*Johnson* v. *Southern Pacific Co.*, 196 U.S. 1, 17 (1904).

[152]*United States* v. *Brown*, 333 U.S. 18, 25 (1948).

[153]*Commonwealth* v. *Jones*, 382 Mass. 387, 391-392 (1981); *Mirageas* v. *Massachusetts Bay Transp. Auth.*, 391 Mass. 815, 819 (1984).

[154]*Rennert* v. *Trustees of State Colleges*, 363 Mass. 740, 743 (1973).

[155]*Cleburne* v. *Cleburne Living Center, Inc.*, 473 U.S. 432, 440 (1985).

[156]*Dunham* v. *State*, 140 Fla. 754 (1939).

[157]*Cleveland* v. *United States*, 329 U.S. 14, 18, 20 (1946).

[158]*Tennessee Valley Auth.* v. *Hill*, 437 U.S. 153, 188 (1978); *Fedorenko* v. *United States*, 449 U.S. 490, 512-513 (1981).

hope that such a theory could be constructed. So far that hope has been disappointed, due at least in part to the preferences of judges. Loose constructionists in the courts (intentionalists) are probably political liberals; strict constructionists (textualists) are probably political conservatives.[159] The methodology of statutory interpretation will probably ebb and flow with the preferences of the judges.[160] Conservatives are not likely to be persuaded that their concern that the legislative will be done may be thwarted, rather than supported, by literalism.[161]

There is not much promise in the suggestions of some scholars ("Three Controversial Theories," *supra*) that the process of statutory interpretation would achieve even-handedness by a judicial exercise similar to the common law privileges of the courts. Even if we assume the constitutionality of those theories—a large assumption, indeed—it is not realistic to assume that legislatures would yield their prerogatives in a cooperative way.

Perhaps the most helpful and practical hope for achieving improvement in the interpretive process lies in proposals that each court system, state and federal, should have a procedure to collate all published judicial opinions in which the reasoning indicates that a particular statute is anachronistic, has problems of constitutional dimension, or lacks drafting precision and clarity. From that material, a committee of the judicial conference of the state or nation might periodically prepare a report and forward it to the appropriate officials or committees of the relevant legislature for their use.[162]

Consistent with these recommendations for coordinated efforts, federal and state attempts have been made to bridge the gap and improve the communication between the courts and the legislatures.[163] Effectiveness of these efforts varies greatly among the several jurisdictions and the probability is that many systems are symbolic rather than effective.

---

[159] See Posner, "Statutory Interpretation—in the Classroom and in the Courtroom," 50 U. Chi. L. Rev. 800, 822 (1983).

[160] For example, see recent cases emphasizing literalness rather than legislative history: *United States* v. *Monsanto*, 491 U.S. 600 (1989) and *Patterson* v. *McLean Credit Union*, 491 U.S. 164 (1989).

[161] See the discussion of this point in the section "Legislative Intent: Plain Meaning," *supra*.

[162] See, e.g., Coffin, "The Problem of Obsolete Statutes: A New Role for Courts?" 91 Yale L.J. 827, 840 (1982).

[163] See Abrahamson and Hughes, "Shall We Dance? Steps for Legislators and Judges in Statutory Interpretation," 75 Minn. L.R. 1045 (1991).

Chief among the impediments to communication is the uncertainty of judges as to their appropriate function in the legislative process.[164]

There is no doubt of the importance of the problems outlined in this chapter. "We have been building up the legislative part of our law in many instances through relatively narrow, more or less detailed responses to particular problems, without taking a general look at what it means to enter upon a legislative system and how we should handle the problems this poses. Such a mode of proceeding could well result, inter alia, in a system difficult to manage because of the legislative burden and insufficient flexibility for sound administration and development."[165]

With no cure-alls in sight, at least we can begin to understand the problems, including the polarity of some judges and the inadequacy of communication between legislatures and courts.

---

[164] *Id.* at 1081-1092.

[165] Kernochan, "Statutory Interpretation: An Outline of Method," 3 Dalhousie L.J. 331, 335 (1976-1977).

Chapter Four

CONSTITUTIONAL LAW

---

1. A Minority View: The Indeterminate Constitution Invalidates Judicial Review

Much of the dialogue as to the meaning of any constitution opposes the original intent of the drafters against present-day political and moral standards. However, there are some scholars who state that the dialogue as to construction of the federal Constitution is a futile exercise; that the Constitution in its open-ended provisions is indeterminate because multiple interpretations are equally supportable, and the conclusions are at the unrestrained choice of the judges.

Some of those who emphasize the indeterminate text especially reject liberal construction of the Constitution, and reject judicial review as invalid. They argue that the Constitution, as construed, is an impediment to progress, as judged by the critics' values. These premises have been called constitutional deconstructionism.[166] (Compare n.14 in Chapter Two, as to Critical Legal Studies.)

2. Constitutional Reasoning in Transition

In the early years of this century, many legal scholars wrote that the law must be adjusted to the real world. Legal process, including constitutional reasoning, had been rule-based, formalistic, and oriented to precedents and logic. The new call was that emphasis should be on the consequences of laws, and some "realists" recognized judges as, not merely law-interpreters, but law-makers. There is no doubt that the realism concept has had in many instances a substantial effect upon judicial reasoning.

Legal realism requires judges to reason like legislators. Inevitably and routinely, certain questions arise: What of the institutional legiti-

---

[166] See, e.g., Tushnet, "Critical Legal Studies and Constitutional Law: An Essay in Deconstruction," 36 Stan. L. Rev. 623 (1984); West, "Constitutional Scepticism," 72 B.U.L. Rev. 765 (1992); Carter, "Constitutional Adjudication and the Indeterminate Text: A Preliminary Defense of an Imperfect Muddle," 94 Yale L.J. 821 (1985) (rejecting "deconstructionism").

---

macy of the courts, the nonmajoritarian branch, in such a process? Is law to be made from the personal views of the judges? What absolutes, what limits, inhibit the courts? These perennial questions are serious enough in the context of the courts' common law function, where the legislature is free to modify or invalidate most judge-made rules of law. They become critical questions in constitutional matters, especially as viewed by strict constructionists. By what privilege, strict constructionists (interpretivists) ask, does the Court presume to satisfy the needs of the real world, by recognizing, as constitutionally protected, certain interests which are not fairly discoverable in the document? The premise is that the restraint and inhibition of the Constitution's language has been impermissibly downgraded.

It is reasonable to conclude that the Supreme Court, in adopting in recent decades some new methodologies of reasoning, has done so in response to a perception that realism in construing the federal Constitution must be coupled with judicial restraint. Thus we have seen a great expansion in reliance on a dual standard of review, with the Court applying strict scrutiny only where there has been intrusion into fundamental rights, or the presence of a suspect classification. We have also seen the adoption of intermediate standards of review, which, even in the development of some matters of social importance, demonstrate the Court's self-restraint in deciding to apply a heightened standard, but something less than strict scrutiny. We have seen the adoption of multipronged formulae which appear to restrain by providing intellectual discipline through formulaic reasoning in certain classes of cases, and we have seen, as to a wide range of constitutional issues, the "balancing" exercises. Balancing of interests clearly identifies the Court with the legislative process, but it can be argued that balancing restrains by requiring a candid disclosure of the Court's reasoning.

The Supreme Court has recognized that state law may provide greater protection for individual rights than the federal Constitution. In recent years, the high courts of states have increasingly relied on state law in the recognition of rights, even in cases where cognate provisions of the federal Constitution were available. This new emphasis on federalism is to some extent a restraining influence on the Supreme Court, especially in instances where the state courts have held the line while the Supreme Court has retreated from previous positions.

We discuss these several restraints in subsequent sections of this chapter. They are clearly far-reaching. Whether they and other restraining influences are intellectually satisfying to all observers is another and serious question.

3. Judicial Restraint: Stare Decisis

We dealt with stare decisis in general terms in our chapter on the common law. We added, in our chapter treating enacted law, some views on precedent that are especially applicable to statutory construction. Recent cases of the Supreme Court have emphasized some views of stare decisis as it relates to constitutional issues. These cases raise the premise that stare decisis, which is designed to promote certainty and stability in the law, may not greatly restrain the judiciary in some constitutional matters.

In 1985, the Supreme Court held that an urban mass-transit authority which received substantial federal monetary assistance, was not immune from federal wage and overtime regulations. In dissent, Justice Rehnquist wrote that the Court's decision violated an established constitutional principle: "...a principle that will, I am confident, in time again command the support of a majority of this Court."[167] This was a clear statement that, with new faces on the court, new interpretation of the Constitution would follow.

There are other recent indications that stare decisis in some instances may have little strength when new justices join the court. In 1991, the Supreme Court, six justices concurring, held that, in the sentencing phase of capital cases, evidence and prosecutorial argument relating to the victim's personal characteristics and the emotional impact of the murder on the victim's family, were admissible.[168] In so doing, the Court overruled a decision it had reached just four years earlier,[169] and another it had reached only two years before.[170]

The Court stated that stare decisis is usually the preferred course, but that the Court had never hesitated to overrule governing decisions which are unworkable or are badly reasoned, and this is particularly

---

[167] *Garcia* v. *San Antonio Metropolitan Transit Auth.*, 469 U.S. 528 (1985). *Garcia* had overruled *National League of Cities* v. *Usery*, 426 U.S. 833 (1976), in which the Court "ruled that the Commerce Clause does not empower Congress to enforce the minimum wage and overtime privisions of the Fair Labor Standards Act (FLSA) against the states 'in areas of traditional governmental functions.'" *Id.* at 530.

[168] *Payne, petitioner* v. *Tennessee*, 111 S. Ct. 2597 (1991).

[169] *Booth* v. *Maryland*, 482 U.S. 496 (1987).

[170] *So. Carolina* v. *Gathers*, 490 U.S. 805 (1989).

true in constitutional cases because in such cases correction through legislation is practically impossible.[171] The Court identified 33 of its previous constitutional decisions which it had overruled in whole or in part in the past 20 terms of the Court.[172]

The Court emphasized that the two cases overruled "were decided by the narrowest of margins, over spirited dissents challenging the basic underpinnings of those decisions."[173] A concurring justice, denying that the Court was exercising "power," stated: "In fact, quite to the contrary, what would enshrine power as the governing principle of this Court is the notion that an important constitutional decision with plainly inadequate rational support must be left in place for the sole reason that it once attracted five votes."[174]

Two justices joined in a dissent which, as to the doctrine of stare decisis, stated: "Neither the law nor the facts supporting *Booth* and *Gathers*, underwent any change in the last four years. Only the personnel of this Court did.... In dispatching *Booth* and *Gathers* to their graves, today's majority ominously suggests that an even more extensive upheaval of this Court's precedents may be in store. Renouncing this Court's historical commitment to a conception of 'the judiciary as a source of impersonal and reasoned judgments,' *Moragne* v. *States Marine Lines*, 398 U.S. 375, 403 ... (1970), the majority declares itself free to discard any principle of constitutional liberty which was recognized or reaffirmed over the dissenting votes of four Justices and with which five or more Justices *now* disagree. The implications of this radical new exception to the doctrine of *stare decisis* are staggering. The majority today sends a clear signal that scores of established constitutional liberties are now ripe for reconsideration; thereby inviting the very type of open defiance of our precedents that the majority rewards in this case."[175]

---

[171] *Payne, supra* at 2609-2610.

[172] *Payne, supra* at 2610, n.1.

[173] *Id.* at 2611.

[174] *Id.* at 2613 (Scalia, J., concurring).

[175] *Id.* at 2619 (Marshall, J., dissenting, joined by Blackmun, J.). In his concurring opinion, *supra* at 2613, Justice Scalia referred to Justice Marshall's statement in *Guardians Ass'n* v. *Civil Serv. Comm'n of New York City*, 463 U.S. 582, 618 (1983) (Marshall, J., dissenting), that the doctrine of stare decisis "is not 'an imprisonment of reason.'" This intra-Court dialogue is more indication that stare decisis is in peril when the faces on the Court change. Compare the statement in *Burnet v. Coronado Oil & Gas Co.*, 285 U.S. 393, 406 (1932) (Brandeis, J., dissenting) that adhering to precedent "is usually the wise policy, because in most matters it is more important that the applicable rule of law be settled than that it be settled right."

4. Judicial Restraint: Interpretivism

There is a school of thought that the Supreme Court has politicized the judicial process by "finding" in the federal Constitution principles which the framers in their general understanding at the time of adoption did not establish.[176] Some who urge restraint in construction are fairly called "literalists" or "textualists" because they look only to the words. Others, called "originalists" or "intentionalists," consider the words and other sources that may assist.[177] At the risk of implying that all who urge restraint are monolithic in their thinking, we refer to them as "interpretivists" and summarize some examples of their views.

Some interpretivists agree that relevant drafting history may properly be considered. Further, although no *new* principle not fairly discoverable in the Constitution may properly be announced, a principle in its definition and application may be modified as time and new circumstances warrant.[178] The premise is that the Supreme Court in exceeding those limits makes moral and political judgments, that this is a legislative and executive function, and consequently the separation of powers and the democratic legitimacy of the court are violated. The interpretivists' claim

---

It has been argued that, solely by reason of changes in the membership of the Court, the "fundamental right" of abortion (*Roe* v. *Wade*, 410 U.S. 113 [1973] and *Thornburgh* v. *American College of Obstetricians & Gynecologists*, 476 U.S. 747 [1986]) is no longer fundamental (see *Webster* v. *Reproductive Health Serv.*, 492 U.S. 490 [1989] and *Planned Parenthood* v. *Casey*, 112 S. Ct. 2791 [1992]). See Allen, "Autonomy's Magic Wand: Abortion and Constitutional Interpretation," 72 B.U.L. Rev. 683, 686 (1992).

[176] See generally, Bork, "The Tempting of America" (1990); Berger, "'Original Intention' in Historical Perspective," 54 Geo. Wash. L. Rev. 296 (1986); Graglia, "Judicial Review on the Bases of 'Regime Principles,'" 26 S. Tex. L. J. 435 (1985); Grano, "Judicial Review and a Written Constitution in a Democratic Society," 28 Wayne L.R. 1 (1981); Berger, "Some Reflections on Interpretivism," 55 Geo. Wash. L.R. 1 (1986); Scalia, "Originalism: the Lesser Evil," 57 U.Cin. L.Rev. 849 (1989).

Compare Meese, "Toward a Jurisprudence of Original Intent," 11 Harv. J.L. & Pub. Pol'y 5 (1988); and Rehnquist, "The Notion of A Living Constitution," 54 Tex. L. Rev. 693 (1976).

[177] There has been a long-standing theoretical discussion whether a Constitution is a statute. That question aside, there clearly are parallels between some theories of statutory construction (see c. 3, §§ 3, 5 and 6, *supra*), and some theories of constitutional construction. See Note: "Justice Scalia's Use of Sources in Statutory and Constitutional Interpretation: How Congress Always Loses," 1990 Duke L.J. 160.

[178] See, e.g., *Katz* v. *United States*, 389 U.S. 347, 353 (1967) (Fourth Amendment applied to electronic surveillance); *Euclid* v. *Ambler Realty Co.*, 272 U.S. 365, 386-387 (1926) ("[W]hile the meaning of constitutional guarantees never varies, the scope of their application must expand or contract to meet the new and different conditions which are constantly coming within the field of their operation").

---

is that the Court has ruled selectively, deciding what results are "good" or "bad," and this process is most clearly for the legislative and executive branches. The process is said to be "political" in that it invokes choices among competitive values or desires. This, say the interpretivists, stands the syllogism on its head, by a process of first deciding the result and then adopting premises to reach the result.

Somewhat related to the interpretivists' thesis is the concept of neutral principles. This states that "the main constituent of the judicial process is that it must be genuinely principled, resting with respect to every step that is involved in reaching judgment on analysis and reasons quite transcending the immediate result that is achieved."[179] The same neutral and principled approach must apply in other analogous cases, again without regard to results. The interpretivist would add that the principle must not only be applied neutrally, but must also be consistent with the framers' intent.

A major interpretivist contention is that the due process clause of the Fifth Amendment, which directs that the federal government must not deprive any person of life, liberty or property without due process of law, requires only that the substance of any law be applied to a person through fair procedures by any tribunal hearing the case. It is denied that the clause is a rule about the allowable substance of a statute. Similarly, the interpretivists' assertion is that the Fourteenth Amendment speaks only to fair procedures in its requirements that the states shall not deprive a person of life, liberty or property without due process of law. Further, that the history of the Fourteenth Amendment shows that its provisions that the states shall not deprive a person of equal protection of the laws was meant only to protect black persons against discrimination. Not only, they say, was equal protection erroneously extended to classifications not involving race, but an equal protection aspect of Fifth Amendment due process, thus applicable to the federal government, was erroneously discovered.[180]

Speaking generally, the interpretivists' position is that, partly as a result of the court's impermissible lodging of substantive content in the due process and equal protection clauses, new constitutional rights have been invented by the Court. In the name of "liberty" and "property"

---

[179] See Wechsler, "Toward Neutral Principles of Constitutional Law," 73 Harv. L. Rev. 1, 15 (1959); Bork, "Neutral Principles and Some First Amendment Problems," 47 Ind. L.J. 1 (1971).

[180] See, e.g., *Bolling* v. *Sharpe*, 347 U.S. 497, 499 (1954).

interests, the Court became the arbiter of the wisdom of statutes aimed at economic regulation.[181] A hitherto undiscovered constitutional right of privacy was found.[182] Some impermissible results were reached which many people would regard as morally and politically "good,"[183] while others were undoubtedly "bad" in the eyes of many or most.[184] Even as to results which were thought to be morally and politically "just," although not "properly" based on principle, the criticism is that the precedential reasoning leads to future mischief.[185]

Some interpretivists read the First Amendment, for example, as protective only of explicit political speech, while conceding that, even as to political speech, some is not constitutionally protected (e.g., speech advocating forcible overthrow of the government).[186]

Debates as to "overreaching" by the judicial branch heightened as the Supreme Court, in a series of cases which some interpretivists say have no support in the Constitution or the Fourteenth Amendment, by "selective incorporation" (a step at a time) has applied portions of the Bill of Rights to the states.[187]

There are emphatic objections to the doctrine of interpretivism. Among these is the view that, as demonstrated in the Court's opinions, principles of relatively recent identification are fairly to be inferred from

---

[181] See, e.g., *Lochner* v. *New York*, 198 U.S. 45 (1905).

[182] See, e.g., *Griswold* v. *Connecticut*, 381 U.S. 479, 484-486 (1965); *Roe* v. *Wade*, 410 U.S. 113 (1973).

[183] See, e.g., *Brown* v. *Board of Educ.*, 347 U.S. 483 (1954).

[184] See, e.g., *Dred Scott* v. *Sandford*, 60 U.S. 393 (1856).

[185] See, e.g., *Bolling* v. *Sharpe*, 347 U.S. 497 (1954). For example, it has been suggested that "legitimate activism" might be based, not on due process or equal protection, but on the Ninth Amendment ("the enumeration in the Constitution of certain rights shall not be construed to deny or disparage others retained by the people"). Bork, "The Supreme Court Needs a New Philosophy," Fortune, Dec. 1968, 138, 168-169.

[186] See generally, Bork, "Neutral Principles and Some First Amendment Problems," 47 Ind. L.J. 1 (1971). Compare *New York Times Co.* v. *Sullivan*, 376 U.S. 254 (1964) (defamation); *Young* v. *American Mini Theatres, Inc.*, 427 U.S. 50 (1976)(content-based restrictions on speech); *Members of City Council* v. *Taxpayers for Vincent*, 466 U.S. 789, 817 (1984) (content-neutral restriction on speech); *Dun & Bradstreet, Inc.* v. *Greenmoss Builders, Inc.*, 472 U.S. 749 (1985) (matter of public concern or of private concern). See also, A. Lewis, "Make No Law" (1991).

[187] See, e.g., Berger, "Some Reflections on Interpretivism," 55 Geo. Wash. L. Rev. 1, 13-15 (1986); L. Pollak, "Original Intention and the Crucible of Litigation," 57 U.Cin.L.Rev. 867 (1989).

reading all of the Constitution's language, not merely a clause at issue.[188] Objection is also offered that the framers' intention cannot be discerned many years later. To this the interpretivist answers that the original understanding is derived effectively and objectively by study of the text, structure and history of the Constitution. Finally, perhaps the principal confrontation with interpretivism offers that our world, our culture, and our problems have changed vastly since the eighteenth century, and the Constitution must also change. We assume that the interpretivists agree that much good, just, and even necessary, law has come from judicial decisions which the interpretivists view as not based on valid constitutional principles. However, the interpretivists add that they appreciate the need for just laws, but these must be achieved democratically by actions of the majoritarian branches, not by overreaching of the courts.

5. Judicial Restraint: Standards of Review, Formulae and Balancing

For many decades the United States Supreme Court had, in pursuit of substantive due process, addressed the constitutionality of statutes concerned with economic regulation. The state was required to demonstrate that its statute pursued an end fairly within the police power and actually contributed to accomplishing its goal. For failure of such proof, the statute was categorized by the Court as without the police power, and thus unconstitutional. These cases are widely criticized as intrusions of the Court into legislative value judgments. *Lochner* v. *New York*[189] is most frequently cited as an example of overreaching by the Court. The formalistic, rule-bound approach of the Court (e.g., *Lochner*) precluded legislative action in many significant matters. Thus, neither Court nor legislature moved effectively in some remedial law, until the advent of realism in recent decades. *West Coast Hotel Co.* v. *Parrish*[190] and *NLRB* v. *Jones & Laughlin Steel Corp.*[191] brought an end to "Lochnerism" and signalled the beginning of a new era of self-imposed restraint by the Court in its constitutional review of acts of the Congress and state legislatures.

---

[188] See the comments of Ely, "Democracy and Distrust," 11-42 (1980), as to the futility ("impossibility") of clause-bound interpretivism.

[189] 198 U.S. 45 (1905).

[190] 300 U.S. 379 (1937).

[191] 301 U.S. 1 (1937).

Standards of Review

The new era of judicial review emphasizes multi-levels of judicial scrutiny. Statutes may be upheld by meeting a mere rationality test, unless they concern a fundamental right or a suspect class. The rationality test is satisfied if the Court can conceive of any logical rationale which the legislature might have considered.[192] Under this test the Court's intrusion into economic regulation has all but disappeared.

Fundamental rights have been described as those explicitly or implicitly established in the Constitution.[193] The Court also has especially recognized as fundamental the right to travel,[194] the right to marry,[195] and the right of access to the courts.[196] Legislation which concerns a fundamental right is subject to strict scrutiny and the government is required to show a compelling governmental interest in the enforcement of the statute.[197]

As to equal protection challenges, there is a similar Court-imposed curb by reason of the Court's adoption of a three-tier system of review. Nearly all statutes engage in some form of classification. The Court has provided special protection against discrimination where a statute classifies by race, alienage, or national origin; statutes which treat these groups (often referred to as "suspect classifications") are subject to strict scrutiny, rather than mere rationality review.[198] *United States* v. *Carolene Prod. Co.*[199] signalled that, not only the suspect classifications but also other "discrete and insular minorities" might be entitled to heightened scrutiny. In this vein the Court not only has recognized the "special

---

[192] See, e.g., *United States* v. *Carolene Prod. Co.*, 304 U.S. 144, 152-154 (1938); and *Commonwealth* v. *Henry's Drywall Co., Inc.*, 366 Mass. 539, 544 (1974).

[193] *San Antonio Indep. Sch. Dist.* v. *Rodriguez*, 411 U.S. 611, 33-34 (1973).

[194] *Shapiro* v. *Thompson*, 394 U.S. 618 (1960).

[195] *Loving* v. *Virginia*, 388 U.S. 611 (1967).

[196] *Boddie* v. *Connecticut*, 401 U.S. 371 (1971).

[197] See, e.g., *Roe* v. *Wade*, 410 U.S. 113, 154-156, 164-165 (1973). See also *Klein* v. *Catalano*, 386 Mass. 701, 712 (1982). The Court has also recognized, in some due process cases, a mid-level review which requires a heightened scrutiny through a balancing test, but does not require the government to demonstrate a compelling state interest. See, e.g., *Youngberg* v. *Romeo*, 457 U.S. 307, 320-321, 324 (1982).

[198] *Cleburne* v. *Cleburne Living Center, Inc.*, 473 U.S. 432, 440 (1985). See, e.g., *In re Griffiths*, 413 U.S. 717, 721-722 (1973); *Fullilove* v. *Klutznick*, 448 U.S. 448 (1980); *Regents of Univ. of Cal.* v. *Bakke*, 438 U.S. 265, 291, 305 (1978); *Plyler* v. *Doe*, 457 U.S. 202, 216 and n.14, 217 and n.15, 218 and n.16, 230 (1982).

[199] 304 U.S. 144, 152-153, n.4 (1938).

status" of claims of discrimination based on gender[200] and legitimacy,[201] but also has established for such cases a middle tier of review between strict scrutiny and mere rationality, whereby it tests whether a statute is substantially related to "important governmental interests."[202]

A methodology in First Amendment cases applies various tests, or levels of scrutiny, to different categories of speech. For example, "The measure of constitutional protection to be afforded commercial speech will surely be governed largely by the content of the communication."[203] Yet, in another case the Court held that the City's interests were sufficiently substantial so as to justify a content-neutral prohibition of posting temporary signs on public property.[204] Commercial speech is at a lower level of protection than some other forms of speech.[205]

While multi-levels of scrutiny set Court-imposed limits upon the Court's constitutional review of legislation, the nature of those limits is determined by the Court's defining and identifying fundamental rights and suspect classes. For example, wealth (or poverty) has not been recognized as "suspect."[206] The conservative jurist presumably would not expand the list of fundamental rights or suspect classes; the liberal jurist presumably would lean toward expansion.

Multi-Pronged Formulae

The Court has established a methodology of review by means of multi-pronged tests or formulae in a wide variety of cases raising constitutional

---

[200] See, e.g., *Craig* v. *Boren*, 429 U.S. 190, 197, 204, 210-212 (1976); *Mississippi Univ. for Women* v. *Hogan*, 458 U.S. 718, 724-725 (1982).

[201] See, e.g., *Lalli* v. *Lalli*, 439 U.S. 259, 265 (1978); and *Trimble* v. *Gordon*, 430 U.S. 762, 766-767, 776 (1977).

[202] See, e.g., *Kramer* v. *Union Free School Dist.*, 395 U.S. 621, 627-628 (1969); *Shapiro* v. *Thompson*, 394 U.S. 618, 634 (1969).

[203] See, e.g., *Young* v. *American Mini Theatres, Inc.*, 427 U.S. 50, 68-69 (1976).

[204] See, e.g., *Members of the City Council* v. *Taxpayers for Vincent*, 466 U.S. 789, 817 (1984).

[205] See, e.g., *Dun & Bradstreet, Inc.* v. *Greenmoss Builders, Inc.*, 472 U.S. 749 (1985).

[206] See Balkin, "The Footnote," 83 Nw. U.L.R. 275 (1989). The author, at 306, 307, identifies four instances where the court did not recognize wealth as a suspect class, and did not recognize the limited political power of the poor: *Dandridge* v. *Williams*, 397 U.S. 471 (1970) (welfare agents); *San Antonio Indep. Sch. Dist.* v. *Rodriguez*, 411 U.S. 1 (1973) (financing of public schools); *Harris* v. *McRae*, 448 U.S. 297 (1980) (financing medically necessary abortion); *New York City Transit Auth.* v. *Beazer*, 440 U.S. 568 (1979) (hiring policies). As to *Rodriguez*, the author especially comments upon the Court's declination to recognize education as a fundamental right, or poverty as a suspect class.

issues, including freedom of speech, right to counsel, search and seizure, procedural due process, and many others.[207]

There is little question that the Court's use of multi-pronged tests tends to support some intellectual discipline, consistency and objectivity in legal analysis. However, the use of such formulae has been criticized as obscuring the constitutional principles behind the mechanics of the analysis.[208]

Balancing

The "balancing" approach is closely related to multi-levels of scrutiny and multi-pronged formulae, indeed appearing sometimes to be simultaneously applied with those techniques. Balancing is probably in recent decades one of the most sweeping innovations in federal constitutional analysis.[209] Traditional legal reasoning is rule-based, concerned with precedent, analogy, syllogistic reasoning and (in constitutional and statutory analysis) drafting history and cultural history. From this reasoning a dialogue evolves as to the meaning of the relevant constitutional principle as applied to the case before the court. By contrast, the balanc-

---

[207] See Nagle, "The Formulaic Constitution," 84 Mich. L. Rev. 165, especially 166-168, and n.3-18 (1985). Professor Nagle offers the following, among many others, as examples of formulae for constitutional review:

The "test" for defining obscenity is: (a) whether "the average person, applying contemporary community standards" would find that the work, taken as a whole, appeals to the prurient interest; (b) whether the work depicts or describes, in a patently offensive way, sexual conduct specifically defined by the applicable state law; and (c) whether the work, taken as a whole, lacks serious literacy, artistic, political, or scientific value. *Miller* v. *California*, 413 U.S. 15, 24 (1973).

The test used to explicate separation of church and state: First, the statute must have a secular legislative purpose; second, its principal or primary effect must be one that neither advances nor inhibits religion; finally, the statute must not foster "an excessive government entanglement with religion." *Lemon* v. *Kurtzman*, 403 U.S. 602, 612-613 (1971).

Heightened scrutiny as to gender discrimination is examined as follows: The party seeking to uphold a statute that classifies individuals on the basis of their gender must carry the burden of showing an "exceedingly persuasive justification" for the classification. The burden is met only by showing at least that the classification serves "important governmental objectives and that the discriminatory means employed" are "substantially related to the achievement of those objectives." [This test] must be applied free of fixed notions concerning the roles and abilities of males and females. Care must be taken in ascertaining whether the statutory objective itself reflects archaic and stereotyping notions. *Mississippi Univ. for Women* v. *Hogan*, 458 U.S. 718, 724, 725 (1982).

[208] *Id.* at 211-212.

[209] See generally, Aleinikoff, "Constitutional Law in the Age of Balancing," 96 Yale L.J. 943 (1987), McFadden, "The Balancing Test," 29 B.C.L.Rev. 585 (1988).

---

ing methodology decides between two alternative results by weighing the competing interests.[210] Although one interest is constitutional, the alternative need not be. For example, the free speech interest in the distribution of handbills may be balanced against the community's interest in clean streets.[211] Also, the individual's protection against unreasonable search and seizure at random highway check-points may be balanced against the public interest in controlling drunken driving.[212] Of course, two constitutional interests may also compete. For example, the perennial confrontation between fair trial and free press, in all its ramifications.[213]

Balancing has been applied to a wide variety of federal constitutional issues. For example, balancing has been frequently applied in First Amendment[214] and Fourth Amendment[215] cases, as well as in cases confronting procedural due process,[216] application of the exclusionary rule under the Fourth Amendment,[217] the commerce clause,[218] and an extraordinary number of cases touching just about all federal constitutional issues.[219] This is not to say that balancing is always applied by the court. Some of the most notable federal constitutional decisions of recent times have been decided without overt indication of balancing.[220]

It is a mistake to think that balancing is confined to constitutional thinking. As we have seen in Chapter Two, *supra*, it has long been entrenched in the courts' thinking on common law. So also, legislatures habitually reach to the outside world to weigh competing interests, and

---

[210]Professor Aleinikoff identifies two types: balancing can be determining if one interest outweighs another, or can be striking a balance between or among competing interests.

[211]*Schneider* v. *State*, 308 U.S. 147, 161 (1939) ("[A] delicate and difficult task falls upon the courts to weigh the circumstances and to appraise the substantiality of the reasons advanced in support of the regulation of the free enjoyment of the rights").

[212]*Delaware* v. *Prouse*, 440 U.S. 648, 653-655 (1979).

[213]*Richmond Newspapers, Inc.* v. *Virginia*, 448 U.S. 555 (1980); *Nebraska Press Ass'n* v. *Stuart*, 427 U.S. 539 (1976); *Sheppard* v. *Maxwell*, 384 U.S. 333 (1966).

[214]See, e.g., *Cantwell* v. *Connecticut*, 310 U.S. 296, 306-307 (1940).

[215]See, e.g., *United States* v. *Place*, 462 U.S. 696, 703 (1983).

[216]See, e.g., *Mathews* v. *Eldridge*, 424 U.S. 319, 334-335 (1976).

[217]See, e.g., *INS* v. *Lopez-Mendoza*, 468 U.S. 1032, 1041 (1984).

[218]See, e.g., *Pike* v. *Bruce Church, Inc.*, 397 U.S. 137, 142 (1970).

[219]See, Aleinikoff, "Constitutional Law in the Age of Balancing," *supra* at n.202, at pages 965, 971.

[220]See, e.g., *Gideon* v. *Wainwright*, 372 U.S. 335 (1963); and *Brown* v. *Board of Educ.*, 347 U.S. 483 (1954).

legislatures have, in statutes, directed the courts to decide issues by a balancing process.[221]

Objections to balancing analysis are many. Some interpretivists may well contest the Court's consideration of non-constitutional interests, and the fact that the weighing process invites the personal value judgments and prejudices of the judge. The contention is that the Court balances as it would in the common law, sometimes disregarding the inhibitions of constitutional language. For example, it is argued (unsuccessfully) that fundamental rights are not susceptible to the balancing exercise.[222]

Other objections offer that the process weighs unlike interests, with no common denominator. Further, the roots of the courts' information as to the outside world may be vague, undisciplined and abstract; the court may rely on litigants' briefs, but may go to the library or other sources for enlightenment as to disciplines other than law. Finally, balancing may establish rules that govern an entire class, where only one member of the class, perhaps unrepresentative, was heard.

The case for balancing is that it is a process inevitably required in interpreting the open ended, much-construed clauses of the Constitution; that it is a response to this century's demand for realism in courts' constitutional reasoning; and that it is this type of reasoning, whether expressed or not, which is almost always used by the Court, and candor requires that it should be expressed.

6. Reliance on State Law

State law may be a catalyst, as well as a precedent, for expansion of federal constitutional rights by the Supreme Court. State law may also provide a buffer against the federal courts' retrenching on their previous construction of constitutional rights. State law may be a source of protection of rights beyond that contained in the federal Constitution.

In 1973, in a case from Texas, the United States Supreme Court heard arguments that public schools in that state should no longer be funded by property taxes assessed by local school districts, because children in less affluent communities were not receiving the equal protection of the laws as required by the federal Constitution. The Supreme Court held that in this context wealth is not a "suspect classification"

---

[221] See, e.g., G.L. c. 208 § 34 (marital property statute [Mass.]).

[222] See, e.g., as to Fourth Amendment rights, *Michigan Dept. of State Police* v. *Sitz*, 496 U.S. 444, 456 (Brennan, J., dissenting), and 460 (Stephens, J., dissenting) (1990).

under the Constitution, is not entitled to heightened scrutiny, and consequently the Texas funding system was not violative of the federal Constitution.[223]

By contrast, in 1989, the high court of Texas held that the state's school financing system violated the state Constitution's equal rights guarantee, stating that "children who live in poor districts must be afforded a substantially equal opportunity to have access to educational funds."[224] The Texas court thus became one of a number of state supreme courts which in recent years reached similar conclusions under their respective state Constitutions.[225]

These results reached by the several state courts illustrate the important principle that state courts acting under state law may extend rights beyond the protection afforded by the federal Constitution. The United States Supreme Court has recognized that this prerogative exists in the states,[226] and that it will not undertake to review the decisions in cases where the state court says "clearly and expressly that it [decision] is alternatively based on bona fide separate, adequate, and independent [state] grounds."[227] Thus the federal Constitution provides only a floor, and not a ceiling, for the protection of rights.

The state ground need not be rooted in the state Constitution; it may come from the state's common law or statute.[228] However, it is clear that in most cases where rights have been extended, the state courts have relied upon the state Constitution.

The state high courts have exercised their prerogative in recent years in a wide variety of cases. Between 1970 and 1989 state courts handed

---

[223] *San Antonio v. Rodriguez*, 411 U.S. 1, 18, 57 (1973).

[224] *Edgewood Indep. Sch. Dist. v. Kirby*, 777 S.W. 2d 391 (Tex. 1989).

[225] See, e.g., *Serrano v. Priest*, 5 Cal. 3d 584 (1971); *Horton v. Meskill*, 172 Conn. 615 (1977); *Robinson v. Cahill*, 62 N.J. 473 (1973); *Dupree v. Alma Sch. Dist.*, 279 Ark. 340 (1983); *Seattle Sch. Dist. v. State*, 90 Wash. 2d 476 (1978); *Washakie Co. Sch. Dist. No. 1 v. Herschler*, 606 P. 2d 310 (Wyo. 1980), cert. denied, 449 U.S. 824 (1980); *Rose v. Council for Better Educ.*, 790 S.W.2d 186 (Ky. 1989); *Helena Elementary Sch. Dist. No. 1 v. State*, 236 Mont. 44 (1989); *McDuffy v. Secretary of the Executive Office of Educ.*, 415 Mass. 545 (1993).

[226] See *Oregon v. Haas*, 420 U.S. 714, 719 (1975); and *Cooper v. California*, 386 U.S. 58, 62 (1967).

[227] *Michigan v. Long*, 463 U.S. 1032, 1041 (1983).

[228] See, e.g., *Guardianship of Roe*, 383 Mass. 415, 417 and n.1, 433 and n.9 (1981) (state ground found in common law control by state court over guardians). Followed in *Mills v. Rogers*, 457 U.S. 291, 301 (1982).

down more than 500 decisions in which they relied on their state Constitutions to provide individual rights protections now lacking under the federal Constitution.[229] Undoubtedly this was caused at least in part by a perception in the states that the Burger and Rehnquist courts have turned away from some of the civil rights decisions of the Warren court.

To illustrate the states' exercise of their prerogatives: the high court of Massachusetts, for example, in civil rights cases has reached beyond federal protection as to issues of search and seizure,[230] sexual and racial discrimination and harassment,[231] capital punishment,[232] state funding of abortions for indigent women,[233] the patient's right to refuse medical treatment even at the peril of death,[234] the patient's right to refuse anti-psychotic medication,[235] the protection of rights of incompetent persons,[236] the right of a political candidate to solicit signatures in a privately owned shopping mall,[237] the sterilization of a retarded and incompetent woman,[238] the protection of persons in certain occupations against mandatory drug testing,[239] and protection against abridgement of the right to free exercise of religion.[240]

Despite the liberal approach of state courts, in many cases, it has been stated that, more often than not, state high courts have followed the lead of the Supreme Court in construing state law that is cognate

---

[229] Linde, "Does the New Federalism Have a Future?" 4 Emerging Issues in State Constitutional Law 251 (1991).

[230] *Commonwealth* v. *Upton*, 394 Mass. 363 (1985).

[231] *O'Connell* v. *Chasdi*, 400 Mass. 686 (1987).

[232] *District Atty. for Suffolk Dist.* v. *Watson*, 381 Mass. 648 (1980).

[233] *Moe* v. *Secretary of Admin. & Fin.*, 382 Mass. 629 (1981).

[234] *Superintendent of Belchertown State Sch.* v. *Saikewicz*, 373 Mass. 728 (1977); and see *Guardianship of Doe*, 411 Mass. 512 (1992).

[235] *Guardianship of Roe*, 383 Mass. 415 (1981).

[236] *Brophy* v. *New England Sinai Hosp., Inc.*, 398 Mass. 417 (1986).

[237] *Batchelder* v. *Allied Stores Int'l, Inc.*, 388 Mass. 83 (1983).

[238] *Matter of Moe*, 385 Mass. 555 (1982).

[239] *Guiney* v. *Police Comm'r of Boston*, 411 Mass. 328 (1991); *O'Connor* v. *Police Comm'r of Boston*, 408 Mass. 324 (1990); and *Horsemen's Benevolent & Protective Ass'n* v. *State Racing Comm'r*, 403 Mass. 692 (1989).

[240] *Society of Jesus* v. *Boston Landmarks Comm'r*, 409 Mass. 38 (1990). Compare *Employment Div., Dept. of Human Resources* v. *Smith*, 494 U.S. 872 (1990) (Supreme Court had provided less protection than the subsequent Massachusetts decision).

with the federal Constitution.[241]

State courts are said to be "laboratories" for the United States Supreme Court to consider on constitutional issues. For example, the high courts of several states held under their state Constitutions several years ago that challenges to jurors cannot be used by the parties in a plan to exclude persons from the jury on account of race, religion or national origin.[242] Later, the Supreme Court, for the first time, held that the federal Constitution forbids a pattern of challenges aimed at racial discrimination in forming a jury.[243] In doing so, the Court expressly followed the lead of the state courts.[244]

It is argued that state courts are the rightful leaders in deciding issues of civil rights because they are closer to the will of the people than are federal judges.[245] This closeness is said to follow from the relative ease with which state law, including state Constitutions, can be amended if the people disagree with their state court. For instance, the people of Massachusetts several years ago voted to amend the state Constitution so as to strike down a holding of the Massachusetts high court[246] that capital punishment was forbidden by the state Constitution. In addition, many states, unlike the federal courts, elect their judges, and the election process is said to be another factor which brings the courts closer to the will of the community.

The fact that state courts may reflect the will of the people may not necessarily be supportive of expanded civil rights. Ours is not merely a democracy; it is a constitutional democracy, with a special purpose of protecting individuals and minority groups. But the majority may not always agree that civil rights should be expanded. The closeness of state courts to the will of the people may serve as a restraint upon some state

---

[241] Latzner, "Into the '90's: More Evidence that the Revolution has a Conservative Underbelly," 4 Emerging Issues in State Constitutional Law 17 (1991). Compare Justice Bennan's emphasis on the importance of state decisions: Brennan, "The Bill of Rights: State Constitutions as Guardians of Individual Rights," 59 N.Y. St. B.J. 10 (1987).

[242] *People* v. *Wheeler*, 22 Cal.3d 258 (1978); *Riley* v. *State*, 496 A.2d 997 (Del. 1985); *State* v. *Neil*, 457 So. 2d 481 (Fla. 1984); *Commonwealth* v. *Soares*, 377 Mass. 461 (1979); *State* v. *Crespin*, 94 N.M. 486 (1980).

[243] *Batson* v. *Kentucky*, 476 U.S. 79, 85-88 (1986).

[244] *Id.* at 82 n.1.

[245] Utter, "State Constitutional Law, The United States Supreme Court, and Democratic Accountability," 64 Wash. L. Rev. 19 (1989).

[246] *District Att'y* v. *Watson*, 381 Mass. 648 (1980); see *Commonwealth* v. *Colon-Cruz*, 393 Mass. 150 (1984).

courts on civil rights issues.

There is at least one other factor which limits the prerogatives of state courts: rights of one party under state law may not be advanced if to do so will undercut the federal constitutional rights of another party.[247]

The increasing importance of state law may not be an unmixed blessing. Variance of law from state to state may have divisive aspects. The advent of new state laws as to abortion is an example. Bitterness on both sides of the controversy, pro-life and pro-choice, may be exacerbated if the exercise of rights are dependent upon the financial ability of a woman to travel to a state of her choice.

7. Interpretation and Application of State Constitutions

There is extraordinary importance in the approach of courts and counsel in analyzing a state constitutional issue, especially in cases where provisions of the state Constitution are in wording identical to, or substantially the same as, cognate federal provisions.[248]

A convincing argument supports the "primacy" method, whereby the state Constitution is analyzed first.[249] The state's law may provide less protection than the federal law, and only then is analysis of the federal law required. However, where state law is proved to be at least as protective as federal law, or more protective, it is unnecessary for the court to examine the federal issue.

A Massachusetts search and seizure case, *Commonwealth* v. *Upton*,[250] illustrates the value of the primacy method. The Massachusetts high court examined the case only under the federal Fourth Amendment and concluded that the search was unlawful.[251] The United States Supreme Court, on appeal by the prosecution, reversed the Massachusetts ruling and held that the search was lawful. A concurring Supreme Court justice stated that the Massachusetts proceeding "reflects an error of a more fundamental character than the one this Court corrects today. It rested

---

[247] See, e.g., *Pruneyard Shopping Center* v. *Robins*, 447 U.S. 74 (1980); *Redgrave* v. *Boston Symphony Orchestra*, 399 Mass. 93 (1987); *Batchelder* v. *Allied Stores Int'l, Inc.*, 388 Mass. 83 (1983).

[248] See, e.g., Utter, "Ensuring Principled Development of State Constitutional Law," 1 Emerging Issues in State Constitutional Law, 217 (1988).

[249] Linde, "First Things First: Rediscovering the States' Bills of Rights," 9 U. Balt. L. Rev. 379 (1980).

[250] 390 Mass. 562 (1983).

[251] *Massachusetts* v. *Upton*, 466 U.S. 727 (1984).

its decision on the Fourth Amendment to the United States Constitution without telling us whether the warrant was valid as a matter of Massachusetts law. It has thereby increased its own burdens as well as ours. For when the case returns to that court, it must then review the probable cause issue once again and decide whether or not a violation of the state constitutional protection against unreasonable searches and seizures has occurred. If such a violation did take place, much of that court's first opinion and all of this Court's opinion are for naught. If no such violation occurred, the second proceeding in that court could have been avoided by a ruling to that effect when the case was there a year ago."[252]

The opinion of the concurring justice was prophetic. The high court of Massachusetts, upon remand of the case, affirmed its original decision, this time under the Massachusetts Constitution, opining that the state Constitution, although nearly identical in wording to the Fourth Amendment, afforded greater protection than its federal counterpart in the determination of probable cause.[253]

Several questions arise from *Upton* and similar cases. Generations of lawyers have habitually failed to raise state law in confronting constitutional issues. Should the state court direct, of its own motion, that the state law issue must be argued, or is this an unwarranted intrusion into the adversarial process? Also, when the state court concludes that it could grant relief under either state or federal law, and then it decides the case using the primacy model, has not the court lost an opportunity for meaningful construction of federal law?

State courts may routinely apply a dual sovereignty analysis, treating both state and federal law, in that order.[254] It has been commented that, if relief is afforded by the first (state law) analysis, what is said in the second (federal law) analysis is dicta. Certainly that is true if, as required by *Michigan* v. *Long*, the state court clearly places its decision upon state law. However, it can also be said that, by expressing its view as to the maximum protection afforded by each Constitution, the state court provides meaningful comment as part of the state-federal dialogue.

In construing state law which is identical or similar in language to wording of the federal Constitution, the state court is of course not

---

[252]*Id*. at 735-736 (Stevens, J., concurring) (fn's deleted).

[253]*Commonwealth* v. *Upton*, 394 Mass. 363, 373 (1985).

[254]See, e.g., Utter, "Ensuring Principled Development of State Constitutional Law," *supra*, 248, 222-224. Justice Utter notes that a dual sovereignty approach which first examines the federal law is referred to as an "interstitial" model.

---

bound by federal interpretation, although federal precedents surely should be respectfully considered along with other authorities, while at the same time stating that the federal cases are not controlling. However, by holdings of the state court, or by amendment of the state Constitution, continuing conformity to the developing federal law (the so-called "lock-step model") may have been adopted as a policy.[255] This constrains the state court, at least in any instance where the state Constitution requires. A question arises, where this "lock-step" model has been adopted by holdings of the state court, whether the state court is in default of its duty to construe the state law independently. Even where the lock-step model has not been adopted, some writers have premised that the state courts are conforming to federal precedent most of the time.[256]

Finally, interpretivists would probably emphasize that construction of the state Constitution should relate to the language of the clause at issue, its context in the document, its drafting history, the relevant history of the state's culture, and any evidence of public policy which pre-existed the document, principally from the common law and statute law of the state.[257] Also, because there is substantial correlation of language in the Constitutions of the several states, meaningful precedents may come from the constructions offered by various state high courts. Included in the discussion of policy may be a weighing of local or state concerns as against the desirability for national uniformity of law.

Interpretivists will argue that without justification rooted in such analysis, some state high courts have found rights greater than those

---

[255] See, e.g., *People* v. *Tisler,* 103 Ill. 2d 226 (1984) (adopting Fourth Amendment doctrine under state Constitution).

[256] From analysis of state constitutional decisions it has been premised that the states are generally conforming to federal precedent. See Latzer, "Into the 90's: More Evidence that the Revolution has a Conservative Underbelly," 4 Emerging Issues in State Constitutional Law 17 (1991).

[257] The high court of Washington stated in *State* v. *Wethereld,* 110 Wash. 2d 466, 472-473 (1988), that it will decline to consider arguments based on the state Constitution unless the advocate discusses at least six factors: "In addition to the textual language itself, we identified the history of the state constitution and common law as important interpretive aids. In addition, we recognized Washington's laws, including statutes, as a source to identify issues of interest to Washington citizens. Matters of particular state or local concern also assist the court in determining whether there is a need for national uniformity or whether that need is outweighed by state policy considerations. In addition, in *Gunwall* we recognized that differences in the text of parallel state and federal constitutional provisions can indicate the state founders intended a meaning different from that of the drafters of the federal Bill of Rights."

protected by the federal Constitution, particularly in cases where the state high court chose not to follow the lead of the Supreme Court in its narrowing of previously recognized federal rights.[258]

In sum, the argument is that principled analysis of the state law issue is required. It follows from such principled approach that identity or similarity of language with the federal Constitution does not necessarily require conformity to federal precedent, nor does a difference in language or history necessarily dictate that the state law affords greater rights than the federal law.

Interpretivists will undoubtedly object to any injection of subjective value judgments by the state court in its construction of state law, perhaps even objecting to a consideration of arguments that good policy and national interest recommend, as to some issues, uniformity of results among the states.

---

[258] See, e.g., *Commonwealth* v. *Upton*, 394 Mass. 363 (1985).

Chapter Five

SOME CONCLUDING THOUGHTS

1. Permanent Tensions

In each of the chapters of this volume we have noted the tensions which intrude in the decision-making functions of judges. Intellectual forces push and pull against each other. By the very nature of our legal system, these tensions will always be with us. Scholarly concern is reflected in thousands of pages, and scores of volumes, which have improved our understanding. Some writers have sought the "quick fix" as to some aspects of legal process, and these approaches are futile exercises. "And the logical method and form flatter that longing for certainty and for repose which is in every human mind. But certainty generally is illusion, and repose is not the destiny of man."[259]

We have seen the tension described, in constitutional dialogue, as between interpretivism and non-interpretivism. Similarly, we have shown that, in statutory construction, the confrontation is between textualism and intentionalism. Some commentators reject both of these schools as "positivistic," and accordingly downgrade the primary role of the legislators as lawmakers.

In more general terms, the tension is phrased as the alignment of the separation of powers against the need for social progress. This phrasing is apt when courts are confronted with public policy issues in the face of legislative inaction or allegedly misdirected action. Similarly, in deciding issues of both common law and constitutional law, the conflict is phrased in terms of formalism, with its emphasis on precedent, and realism, with its emphasis on consequences.

The most acute of all tensions is the confrontation in decision-making between objectivity and the judge's personal philosophy. The judge's personal views (the "can't helps" to which O. W. Holmes and Paul Freund referred) are consistently present, at least as potential influences in decisions. Confrontation is often between political liberalism and

---

[259] Holmes, "The Path of the Law," 10 Harv. L. Rev. 457, 466 (1897).

political conservatism.[260] In Chapter One of this volume we spoke of institutional legitimacy of the courts. This is more than a theoretical concern. Just as public unrest may follow when a president of the United States is charged with exceeding his constitutional powers, so opposition to any decision of a court may focus not only on the merits but on the doubtful source of the court's power.

2. Selection of Judges

The great power of judges in making law, and in reviewing the acts of the other branches for constitutionality, lends extraordinary importance to the judicial selection process. Rhetorical devices in judicial opinions[261] cannot obscure the great power of the courts. It is futile to hope that the courts' decisions will invariably be an expression of popular opinion.[262] When we consider the courts' function in the context of majority rule and minority rights, broad power in the nonmajoritarian branch is a given in the common law, and especially in constitutional law.

There probably never will be an end to the debate between the proponents of the election of judges and those who favor the appointment system.[263] We assume that there is common agreement that, under either method of selection, the best qualified persons should be identified and chosen. Beyond that agreement upon quality, the debate continues.[264]

The principal argument for election of judges is that the election process is consistent with democratic government. The great power exerted by judges is cited as the best reason why they should be chosen

---

[260]"It may therefore be said that the most important thing about a judge is his philosophy and if it be dangerous for him to have one, it is at all events less dangerous than the self-deception of having none." Freund, "Social Justice," 93, 110 (1962).

[261] For example, a court stating or implying, in announcing new law, that it is merely identifying law that has long been there. Bacon says that a court thus contrives "by show of antiquity, to introduce novelty." "Essays of Bacon," Peter Pauper Edition.

[262]This hope that the law-making power of the nonmajoritarian branch can be accommodated in a democracy has been expressed as follows: "This, [acceptance of the courts' decisions by the community] in the end is how and why judicial review is consistent with the theory and practice of political democracy." Bickel, "The Least Dangerous Branch" 258 (2d 1962). But see Fallon, "Of Speakable Ethics and Constitutional Law," 56 U.Chi.L.Rev. 1523, 1540-1543 (consensus view of ethics and morality may be impossible to determine). Compare n. 45, *supra*.

[263]We noted in Chapter One, Section Two, that even in an elective system, judges first take office by appointment.

[264]Author's note: I am convinced that the appointive system is the better method, but I have attempted to be even-handed in stating the opposing arguments.

by the voters. See the related discussion in Section Two of Chapter One ("The Courts are Nonmajoritarian") that the people will not be content with a "legislature" of seven or nine members. The contention is that fears of injustice to minorities, and fears of partiality related to campaign contribution, are not based in reality or fact. Finally, the superiority claimed for the appointive system has weight only if appointments are keyed to excellence and are not themselves politicized.

The case for appointment of judges observes that ours is not only a democracy; it is a constitutional democracy. The argument that elected judges are more likely to reflect the will of the majority of the people is countered with the assertion that the rights of individuals and minorities may be neglected or abused in an elective system. One of the central arguments in the pre-Constitution debates of the eighteenth century was that in a democracy the strong would devour the weak. This fear is best met, as in the federal Constitution, by establishing an independent judiciary, immune from the election process. "Our commitment to self-government in a representative government must be reconciled with vesting in electorally unaccountable Justices the power to invalidate the expressed desires of representative bodies on the grounds of inconsistency with higher law."[265] Stated another way, decisions of appointed judges are not affected by fear of the next election. Further argument is that campaign fund-raising by judges, especially solicitation from lawyers and law firms, is challenged as inconsistent with the impartiality required of judges. It is also offered that voters are seldom if ever well informed as to the special qualities required in a competent judge.

Some states have taken a mid-position in requirements that judges must be reappointed periodically by the then governor (e.g. every seven years). This process, while it may not and probably should not confront the subtleties of the judge's legal or political philosophy, may serve to weed out the judge who has performed unsatisfactorily but not so badly as to be susceptible to the extraordinary process of impeachment.

Whatever the method of selection, it is crystal clear that it makes a massive difference to the community "how well [judges and lawyers] understand judging in our legal system and what [they] believe about commitment to professionalism and method in judging."[266] It is true, as we have emphasized throughout these pages (see especially "Permanent Tensions," above), that we lack certainty of method and rules of

---

[265] Brennan, "Interpreting the Constitution," Social Policy, Summer 1987, 24-25.
[266] Keeton, "Judging," at 261 (1990).

interpretation in the common law, statute law and constitutional law. These uncertainties of method demonstrate the need for excellence in the judiciary. To the extent that objectivity in decision making is sometimes replaced by the judge's personal choice of values, the need for a process that identifies and chooses judges of character and experience is underlined.[267] From all that we have said in this volume, we begin to appreciate the words of Justice Holmes: "The life of the law has not been logic; it has been experience."[268] Perhaps, from all that Holmes has written, and from our analysis in this volume, the more accurate statement is that the life of the law has been both logic and experience.

Ultimately, of course, and beyond the selection process, success in our justice system depends upon the judges' performance. "In searching for perfect justice, we seek the impossible, but the search is worth our total efforts. What we in the courts do, and how we do it, is seen not only by the litigants before us, but by the entire community. The stakes are high. Our performance will help to determine whether constitutional principles are nourished and whether human rights are advanced."[269]

---

[267] See, e.g., Tushnet, "Constitutional Interpretation, Character and Experience," 72 B.U.L. Rev. 747 (1992).

[268] Holmes, "The Common Law" 1 (1881). See the related statement of Holmes, *supra* c. 1, n. 40, that judges know too much to sacrifice common sense to a syllogism.

[269] Excerpt from remarks by E. F. Hennessey on April 22, 1982, at memorial services for a distinguished judicial colleague, Honorable Paul G. Kirk.

TABLE OF RELEVANT WRITINGS

This is a listing of materials selected from the great number of writings concerned with the decision-making process. Most of these materials appear in our footnotes in the text. Several of them are so broad in their discussion that we list them under both common law and constitutional law.

Common Law

Abraham, H.
"Freedom and the Court" (4th ed. 1982)

Aldisert, R.
"Logic for Lawyers" (1989)

Auerbach, C.
"A Revival of Some Ancient Learning: A Critique of Eisenberg's 'The Nature of the Common Law,'" 5 Minn.L.Rev. 539 (1991)

Balkin, J.
"The Crystalline Structure of Legal Thought," 39 Rutgers L.Rev. 1 (1986)

Bell, J.
"Policy Arguments in Judicial Decisions" (1983)

Boyle, J.
"The Politics of Reason, Critical Legal Studies and Second Thoughts," 133 U.Pa.L.Rev. 685 (1985)

Cardozo, B.
"The Nature of the Judicial Process" (1921)
"The Paradoxes of Legal Science" (1928)

Caudill, D.
"Disclosing Tilt: A Partial Defense of Critical Legal Studies and a Comparative Introduction to the Philosophy of Law-Idea," 71 Iowa L.Rev. 287 (1987)

Coffin, F.
"The Ways of a Judge" (1980)

Cohen, J.
"Ethical Systems and Legal Ideals" (1959)
Dewey, J.
"Logical Method and Law," 10 Cornell L.Q. 17 (1924)
Dworkin, R.
"Taking Rights Seriously" (1977)
Eisenberg, M.
"The Nature of the Common Law" (1988)
Epstein, R.
"The Social Consequences of Common Law Rules," 95 Harv.L.Rev. 1717 (1982)
Fallon, R.
"Of Speakable Ethics and Constitutional Law: A Review Essay," 56 U.Chi.L.Rev. 1523 (1989)
Feinberg, J.
"Justice, Fairness and Rationality," 81 Yale L.J. 1004 (1972)
Freund, P.
"Social Justice" (1962)
Fiss, O.
"Objectivity and Interpretation," 34 Stan.L.Rev. 739 (1982)
Flynn, J.
"A Comment on 'The Common Law Origins of the Infield Fly Rule,'" 4 J.Contemp.L. 241 (1978)
Frank, J.
"Law and the Modern Mind" (1970)
Fuller, L.
"The Morality of Law" (rev. ed. 1969)
Gilmore, G.
"The Age of Anxiety," 84 Yale L.J. 1022 (1975)
Greenawalt, K.
"The Enduring Significance of Neutral Principles," 78 Colum.L.Rev. 982 (1978)
Grib, P.
"The Ethical Foundations of Judicial Decision-Making," 35 Cath. Law. 1 (1993)
Harris, J.
"Legal Philosophies" (1980)

Hart, H.

"The Concept of Law" (1961)

"Essays on Bentham: Jurisprudence and Political Theory" (1982)

"Positivism and the Separation of Law and Morals," 71 Harv.L.Rev. 593 (1958)

Hart, A. and Sacks, A.

"The Legal Process: Basic Problems in the Making and Application of Law," (tent. ed., Cambridge, 1958)

Heineman, B.

"A Balance Wheel on the Court," 95 Yale L.J. 1325 (1985)

Holmes, O.W.

"The Common Law" (1881)

"Law in Science - Science in Law" (1920)

"The Path of the Law," 10 Harv.L.Rev. 457 (1897)

Hutcheson, J.

"The Judgment Intuitive: The Function of the 'Hunch' in Judicial Decisions," 14 Cornell L.Q. 274 (1919)

Hutchinson, A. and Monahan, P.

"Law Politics and the Critical Legal Scholars: The Unfolding Drama of American Legal Thought," 36 Stan.L.Rev. 199 (1984)

Kornhauser, L.

"A Guide to the Perplexed Claims of Efficiency in the Law," 8 Hofstra L.Rev. 591 (1980)

Keeton, R.

"Judging" (1990)

Levi, E.

"An Introduction to Legal Reasoning" (1949)

Llewellyn, K.

"The Common Law Tradition: Deciding Appeals" (1960)

Luhmann, N.

"A Sociological Theory of Law" (1985)

Luizzi, V.

"Balancing of Interests in Courts," 20 Jurimetrics J. 373 (1980)

McFadden, P.

"The Balancing Test," 29 B.C.L.Rev. 585 (1988)

Milsom, S.

"Historical Foundations of the Common Law" (2nd ed. 1981)

Moore, M.

"The Semantics of Judging," 54 S.Cal.L.Rev. 151 (1981)

Note: "The Common Law Origins of the Infield Fly Rule," 4 J.Contemp.L. 233 (1978)

Note: "'Round and 'Round the Bramble Bush: From Legal Realism to Critical Legal Studies," 95 Harv.L.Rev. 1 (1982)

O'Connell, K.

"Taking Process Seriously in Judicial Decision Making," 67 Or.L.Rev. 837 (1988)

Perry, J.

"Morality, Politics, and Law: A Bicentennial Essay" (1988)

Posner, R.

"The Problems of Jurisprudence" (1990)

Postema, G.

"Bentham and the Common Law Tradition" (1986)

Pound, R.

"The Judicial Process in Action," 1 N.Y.L. Forum (1955)

"Liberty of Contract," 18 Yale L.J. 454 (1909)

"Mechanical Jurisprudence," 8 Colum.L.Rev. 605 (1908)

"A Survey of Social Interests," 57 Harv.L.Rev. 1 (1943)

"The Theory of Judicial Decision," 36 Harv.L.Rev. 940 (1923)

Radin, J.

"Reconsidering the Rule of Law," 69 B.U.L.Rev. 781 (1989)

Rawls, J.

"A Theory of Justice" (1971)

Raz, J.

"The Authority of Law" (1979)

Redish, M.

"The Value of Free Speech," 130 U.Pa.L.Rev. 591 (1982)

Richards, D.

"Rules, Policies and Neutral Principles: The Search for Legitimacy in Common Law and Constitutional Adjudication," 11 Ga.L.Rev. 1069 (1977)

Scalia, A.

"The Rule of Law as a Law of Rules," 56 U.Chi.L.Rev. 1175 (1989)

Schauer, F.

"Is the Common Law Law?," 77 Cal.L.Rev. 455 (1989)

Sheldon, C.

"The American Judicial Process: Models and Approaches" (1974)

Summers, R.

"Two Types of Substantive Reasons: The Core of a Theory of Common-Law Justification," 63 Cornell L.Rev. 707 (1978)

Soper, P.

"A Theory of Law" (1984)

Twining, W.

"Karl Llewellyn and the Realist Movement" (1973)

Unger, R.

"The Critical Legal Studies Movement" (1986)

"Law in Modern Society" (1976)

Wasserstrom, R.

"The Judicial Decision" (1961)

Weinreg, L.

"Natural Law and Justice" (1987)

Wellington, H.

"Common Law Rules and Constitutional Double Standards: Some Notes on Adjudication," 83 Yale L.J. 221 (1973)

White, J.

"The Legal Imagination" (1973)

Wilkinson, J.

"The Role of Reason in the Rule of Law," 56 U.Chi.L.Rev. 779 (1989)

Wittgenstein, L.

"Philosophical Investigations" (1968)

Yablon, C.

"Justifying the Judge's Hunch: An Essay on Discretion," 41 Hastings L.J. 231 (1990)

Enacted Law

Abrahamson, S. and Hughes, R.
"Shall We Dance? Steps for Legislators and Judges in Statutory Interpretation," 75 Minn.L.Rev. 1045 (1991)

Aleinikoff, T.
"Updating Statutory Interpretation," 87 Mich.L.Rev. 20 (1988)

Atiyah, R. and Summers, R.
"Form and Substance in Anglo-American Law: A Comparative Study in Legal Reasoning, Legal Theory, and Legal Institutions" (1987)

Blatt, W.
"The History of Statutory Interpretation: A Study in Form and Substance," 7 Cardozo L.Rev. 799 (1985)

Calabresi, G.
"A Common Law for the Age of Statutes" (1982)

Coffin, F.
"The Problem of Obsolete Statutes: A New Role for the Courts?" 91 Yale L.J. 827 (1982)

DeMuth, C. and Ginsburg, D.
"White House Review of Agency Rulemaking," 99 Harv.L.Rev. 1075 (1986)

DeSloovere, F.
"The Equity and the Reason of the Statute," 21 Cornell L.Q. 591 (1936)

Dickerson, R.
"The Interpretation and Application of Statutes" (1975)

Diver, C.
"Policymaking Paradigms in Administrative Law," 95 Harv.L.Rev. 393 (1981)

Dworkin, R.
"Law's Empire" (1986)

Easterbrook, F.
"Legal Interpretation and the Power of the Judiciary," 7 Harv.J.L. & Pub. Pol'y 871 (1984)
"Forward: The Court and the Economic System," 98 Harv.L.Rev. 1 (1984)

Eisenberg, M.
"The Nature of the Common Law" (1988)

Endlich, G.
"A Commentary on the Interpretation of Statutes" (1988)

Epstein, R.
"The Pitfalls of Interpretation," 7 Harv.J.L. & Pub. Pol'y 101 (1984)

Eskridge, W. and Frickey, P.
"Cases and Materials on Legislation; Statutes and the Creation of Public Policy" (1988)

Finkelstein, J.
"In re Brett: The Sticky Problem of Statutory Construction," 52 Fordham L.Rev. 430 (1983)

Frankfurter, F.
"Some Reflections on the Reading of Statutes," 47 Colum.L.Rev. 527 (1947)

Freedman, J.
"Crisis and Legitimacy: The Administrative Process and American Government" (1978)

Friendly, H.
"Benchmarks" (1967)

Fuller, L.
"Positivism and Fidelity to Law," 71 Harv.L.Rev. 630 (1958)

Gelhorn, E. and Robinson, G.
"Rulemaking 'Due Process': An Inconclusive Dialogue," 48 U.Chi.L.Rev. 201 (1981)

Hart, H.
"Positivism and the Separation of Law and Morals," 71 Harv.L.Rev. 593 (1958)

Hart, H. and Sacks, A.
"The Legal Process: Basic Problems in the Making and Application of Law," 1201 (tent. ed., Cambridge, 1958)

Holmes, O.W.
"The Theory of Legal Interpretation," 12 Harv.L.Rev. 417 (1899)

Horwitz, M.
"The Transformation of American Law" (1977)

Kernochan, J.
"Statutory Interpretation: An Outline of Method," 3 Dalhousie L.J. 331 (1976-1977)

Linde, H.
"Due Process of Lawmaking," 55 Neb.L.Rev. 197 (1976)

Llewellyn, K.
"Remarks on Theory of Appellate Decision," 3 Vand.L.Rev. 395 (1950)

Morrison, A.

"OMB Interference with Agency Rulemaking: The Wrong Way to Write a Regulation," 99 Harv.L.Rev. 1059 (1986)

Note: "Intent, Clear Statements, and the Common Law; Statutory Interpretation in the Supreme Court," 95 Harv.L.Rev. 892 (1982)

Note: "The Use of Extrinsic Aids in the Interpretation of Popularly Enacted Legislation," 89 Colum.L.Rev. 157 (1989)

Posner, R.

"Economics, Politics and the Reading of Statutes and the Constitution," 49 U.Chi.L.Rev. 263 (1982)

"Statutory Interpretation in the Classroom and in the Courtroom," 50 U.Chi.L.Rev. 800 (1983)

Pound, R.

"Spurious Interpretations," 7 Colum.L.Rev. 379 (1907)

Radin, M.

"Statutory Interpretation," 43 Harv.L.Rev. 863 (1930)

Rodriguez, D.

"The Substance of the New Legal Process," 77 Cal.L.Rev. 919 (1989)

Rose-Ackerman, S.

"Progressive Law and Economics—and the New Administrative Law," 98 Yale L.J. 341 (1988)

Smith, S.

"Law Without Mind," 88 Mich.L.Rev. 104 (1989)

Stewart, P.

"The Reformation of American Administrative Law," 88 Harv.L.Rev. 1667 (1975)

Sunstein, C.

"In Defense of the Hard Look: Judicial Activism and Administrative Law," 7 Harv.J.L. & Pub. Pol'y 51 (1984)

Vining, J.

"The Authoritative and the Authoritarian" (1986)

Weisberg, R.

"The Calabresian Judicial Artist: Statutes and the New Legal Process," 35 Stan.L.Rev. 213 (1983)

Williams, B.

"Dworkin on Community and Critical Interests," 77 Cal.L.Rev. 515 (1989)

Constitutional Law

Abraham, J.
"Justices and Presidents: A Political History of Appointments to the Supreme Court" (1985)

Ackerman, B.
"Reconstructing American Law" (1984)
"Social Justice and the Liberal State" (1980)
"We the People" (1991)

Aleinikoff, T.
"Constitutional Law in the Age of Balancing," 96 Yale L.J. 943 (1987)

Balkin
"The Footnote," 83 Nw. U.L.Rev. 275 (1989)

Berger, R.
"Against an Activist Court," 31 Cath.U.L.Rev. 173 (1982)
"Federalism: The Founders' Design" (1987)
"Government by Judiciary: The Transformation of the Fourteenth Amendment" (1977)
"New Theories of 'Interpretation': The Activist Flight from the Constitution," 47 Ohio St.L.J. 1 (1986)
"'Original Intention' in Historical Perspective," 54 Geo.Wash.L.Rev. 296 (1986)
"Some Reflections on Interpretivism," 55 Geo.Wash.L.Rev. 1 (1986)

Bickel, A.
"The Least Dangerous Branch" (2d ed. 1962)

Bork, R.
"The Constitution, Original Intent, and Economic Rights," 23 San Diego L.Rev. 823 (1986)
"Neutral Principles and Some First Amendment Problems," 47 Ind.L.J. 1 (1971)
"The Tempting of America" (1990)

Brennan, W.
"In Defense of Dissents," 37 Hastings L.J. 426 (1986)
"Interpreting the Constitution," 24 Social Policy (Summer 1987)
"Some Judicial Aspects of Federalism," 52 Rev. Jur. U.P.R. 1 (1983)
"The Criminal Prosecution: Sporting Event or Quest for Truth? A Progress Report," 68 Wash. U.L.Q. 1 (1990)
"Reason, Passion, and 'The Progress of the Law,'" 10 Cardozo L.Rev. 3 (1988)

"The Bill of Rights: State Constitution as Guardians of Individual Rights," 59 N.Y.St. B.J. 10 (1987)

"The Equality Principle in American Constitutional Jurisprudence," 48 Ohio St.L.J. 921 (1987)

"My Encounter with the Constitution," 26 Judges' J. 7 (1987)

Brest, P.

"The Fundamental Rights Controversy: The Essential Contradictions of Normative Constitutional Scholarship," 90 Yale L.J. 1063 (1981)

"The Misconceived Quest for the Original Understanding," 60 B.U.L.Rev. 204 (1980)

Carter, S.

"The Constitutional Adjudication and the Indeterminate Text: A Preliminary Defense of an Imperfect Muddle," 94 Yale L.J. 821 (1985)

Choper, J.

"Judicial Review and the National Process: A Functional Reconsideration of the Role of the Supreme Court" (1980)

Douglas, C.

"State Judicial Activism—The New Role for State Bills of Right," 12 Suffolk U.L.Rev. 1123 (1978)

Dworkin, R.

"Law's Empire" (1987)

"Liberal Community," 77 Cal.L.Rev. 479 (1989)

"The Theory and Practice of Autonomy" (1988)

"Taking Rights Seriously" (1977)

Esterbrook, F.

"Method, Result, and Authority: A Reply," 98 Harv.L.Rev. 622 (1985)

Ely, J.

"Democracy and Distrust: A Theory of Judicial Review" (1980)

Fairman, C.

"Does the Fourteenth Amendment Incorporate the Bill of Rights? The Original Understanding," 2 Stan.L.Rev. 5 (1949)

Fallon, R.

"Of Speakable Ethics and Constitutional Law: A Review Essay," 56 U.Chi.L.Rev. 1523 (1989)

Feinberg, J.

"Harm to Self" (1986)

Field, O.

"The Advisory Opinion—An Analysis," 24 Ind.L.J. 203 (1949)

Finnis, J.

"Natural Law and Natural Rights" (1980)

Frantz, L.

"The First Amendment in the Balance," 71 Yale L.J. 1424 (1962)

Fried, C.

"Two Concepts of Interests: Some Reflections on the Supreme Court's Balancing Test," 76 Harv.L.Rev.755 (1963)

Glendon, M.

"Abortion and Divorce in Western Law" (1987)

Graglia, L.

"Judicial Review on the Basis of 'Regime Principles': A Prescription for Government by Judges," 26 S.Tex.L.J. 435 (1985)

Grano, J.

"Judicial Review and a Written Constitution in a Democratic Society," 28 Wayne L.R. 1 (1981)

Hart, H.

"The Concept of Law" (1961)

Henkin, L.

"Infallibility Under Law: Constitutional Balancing," 78 Colum.L.Rev. 1022 (1978)

Irons, P.

"Making Law: The Case for Judicial Activism," 24 Val.U.L.Rev. 35 (1989)

Latzner, B.

"Into the '90's: More Evidence that the Revolution has a Conservative Underbelly," 4 Emerging Issues in State Constitutional Law (1991)

Lewis, A.

"Make No Law" (1991)

Linde, H.

"Does the New Federalism Have a Future?" 4 Emerging Issues in State Constitutional Law 251 (1991)

"E Pluribus—Constitutional Theory and State Courts," 18 Ga.L.Rev. 165 (1984)

"First Things First: Rediscovering the States' Bills of Rights," 9 U.Balt.L.Rev. 379 (1980)

Llewellyn, K.

"Some Realism About Realism—Responding to Dean Pound," 44 Harv.L.Rev. 1222 (1934)

Mashaw, J.

"The Supreme Court's Due Process Calculus for Administrative Adjudication in *Mathews* v. *Eldridge*: Three Factors in Search of a Theory of Value," 44 U.Chi.L.Rev. 28 (1976)

Meese, E.

"Toward a Jurisprudence of Original Intent," 11 Harv.J.L. & Pub. Pol'y 5 (1988)

Mendelson, W.

"On the Meaning of the First Amendment: Absolutes in the Balance," 50 Cal.L.Rev. 821 (1962)

McFadden, P.

"The Balancing Test," 29 B.C.L.Rev. 585 (1988)

Moore, M.

"Three Concepts of Rules," 14 Harv.J.L. & Pub. Pol'y 771 (1991)

Nagle, T.

"The Formulaic Constitution," 84 Mich.L.Rev. 165 (1985)

Note: "The Case for an Advisory Function in the Federal Judiciary," 50 Geo.Wash.L.J. 785 (1962)

Note: "The Civil and Criminal Methodologies of the Fourth Amendment," 93 Yale L.J. 1127 (1984)

O'Connell, K.

"Taking Process Seriously in Judicial Decision Making," 67 Or.L.Rev. 837 (1988)

Perry, J.

"Morality, Politics, and Law: A Bicentennial Essay" (1988)

Perry, M.

"The Constitution, the Courts and Human Rights" (1982)

Pollak, L.

"'Original Intention' and the Crucible of Litigation," 57 U.Cin. L.Rev. 867 (1989)

Radin, M.

"Reconsidering the Rule of Law," 69 B.U.L.Rev. 781 (1989)

Rawls, J.

"A Theory of Justice" (1971)

Regan, D.

"The Supreme Court and State Protectionism: Making Sense of the Dormant Commerce Clause," 84 Mich.L.Rev. 1091 (1986)

Rehnquist, W.

"The Notion of a Living Constitution," 54 Tex.L.Rev. 693 (1976)

Scalia, A.

"Originalism: the Lesser Evil," 57 U.Cin.L.Rev. 849 (1989)

Schauer, F.

"Playing by the Rules: A Philosophical Examination of Rule-Based Decision-Making in Law and in Life" (1991)

Seidman, L.

"Public Principle and Private Choice: The Uneasy Case for a Boundary Maintenance Theory of Constitutional Law," 96 Yale L.J. 1006 (1987)

Shiffrin, S.

"The First Amendment and Economic Regulation: Away from a General Theory of the First Amendment," 78 Nw.U.L.Rev. 1212 (1983)

Sunstein, C.

"Lochner's Legacy," 87 Colum.L.Rev. 873 (1987)

Tribe, L.

"Constitutional Calculus: Equal Justice or Economic Efficiency," 98 Harv.L.Rev. 592 (1985)

Tribe, L. and Dorf, M.

"On Reading the Constitution" (1991)

Tushnet, M.

"Following the Rules Laid Down: A Critique of Interpretivism and Neutral Principles," 96 Harv.L.Rev. 781 (1983)

"Critical Legal Studies and Constitutional Law: An Essay in Deconstruction," 36 Stan.L.Rev. 623 (1984)

Twining, W.

"Karl Llewellyn and the Realist Movement" (1973)

Utter, R.

"Ensuring Principled Development of State Constitutional Law," 1 Emerging Issues in State Constitutional Law 217 (1988)

"State Constitutional Law, the United States Supreme Court, and Democratic Accountability," 64 Wash.L.Rev. 19 (1989)

Wasserstrom, S. and Seidman, L.

"The Fourth Amendment as Constitutional Theory," 77 Geo.Wash.L.J. 19 (1988)

Wechsler, H.

"Toward Neutral Principles of Constitutional Law," 73 Harv.L.Rev. 1 (1959)

Weinreg, L.
"Natural Law and Justice" (1987)

West, R.
"Constitutional Skepticism," 72 B.U.L.Rev. 765 (1992)

Wilkinson, J.
"The Role of Reason in the Rule of Law," 56 U.Chi.L.Rev. 779 (1989)

Yablon, C.
"Justifying the Judge's Hunch: An Essay on Discretion," 41 Hastings L.J. 231 (1990)

ABOUT THE AUTHOR

Edward F. Hennessey served for 18 years as a Justice of the Supreme Judicial Court of Massachusetts, and for the last 13 of those years he was Chief Justice of that court (1976-1989). For five years (1967-1971) he was a trial judge in the Superior Court of Massachusetts, after a law practice as a trial attorney in both civil and criminal cases. He was President of the National Conference of Chief Justices (1985-1986) and President of the National Center for State Courts.

ABOUT THE
FLASCHNER JUDICIAL INSTITUTE

Established in 1978, the Institute is a memorial to the late Chief Justice of the Massachusetts District Courts, Hon. Franklin N. Flaschner—a man beloved by many and admired by all for his dedication to judicial education. "Apart from the judicial selection process," the Chief Justice once noted, "the most meaningful factor in improving professionalism is commitment to judicial education."

Frequently characterized as a "self-help judges' organization," the Flaschner Judicial Institute is organized as a not-for-profit Massachusetts corporation and it is exempt from federal taxes. In 1990, the Flaschner Judicial Institute won the American Bar Association's coveted "State Judicial Education Award," given to the nation's most outstanding educational organization serving a state judiciary. The Institute enjoys the continuing support of the Massachusetts Bar Foundation.

For more information about the Flaschner Judicial Institute, please contact: Robert J. Brink, Executive Director, 10 Winter Place, Boston, MA 02108. Tel: (617) 542-8838 Fax: (617) 542-7280

The typeface used in this book is Galliard. It is based on a type made by Robert Granjon in the sixteenth century and is the first typeface to be designed for phototypesetting.

The book was typeset, printed, and bound by The Studley Press, Dalton, Massachusetts. The cover is printed on Simpson Gainsborough and the text is printed on Mohawk Vellum.